PEOPLE IN CHARGE

Creating Self Managing Workplaces

Robert Rehm

Hawthorn Press

People in Charge Copyright © 1999 Robert Rehm

Robert Rehm is hereby identified as author of this work in accordance with Section 77 of the Copyright, Designs and Patent Act, 1988. He asserts and gives notice of his moral right under this Act.
Individual case studies copyright of respective authors.

Published by Hawthorn Press, Copyright © 1999
Hawthorn House, 1 Lansdown Lane, Stroud, Gloucestershire,
GL5 1BJ. Gt Britain
Tel. (01453) 757040   Fax. (01453) 751138
E-mail: hawthornpress@hawthornpress.com

Cover design by Patrick Roe, Southgate Solutions
Illustrations by Abigail Large
Typeset at Hawthorn Press by Frances Fineran
Printed by Redwood Books, Trowbridge, Wiltshire

Front cover photograph and photographs in Chapter 6 reproduced by kind permission of South African Land Bank. Back cover photograph of the author is by Vann Hilty. Photographs in Chapter 11 reproduced by kind permission of Allan Kobernick. Photographs in Chapter 13 reproduced by kind permission of Dianne Baasch.

A catalogue record of this book is available from the British Library Cataloguing in Publication Data

ISBN 1 869 890 87 6

'This is not one of those boring, stodgy management theory books. With rich accounts of real life organisations that vary from high tech electronics assembly to a chamber orchestra, this book gives novice and experienced self management advocates a peek behind the scenes of what makes self managing organisations work, and what makes them fail. In crisp no-nonsense language this book shows how to move from a traditional organisational structure to one comprised entirely of highly motivated, high performing self managing teams.'

Tom Devane, Co-author, *The Change Handbook: Group Methods for Shaping the Future*

'Self managing workplaces offer the holy grail of organisational development – greater responsibility and teamwork, reduced costs and cycle time. But like the quest for the grail itself, the difficulty lies in the journey as the organisation is forced to confront its own patterns and prejudices. *People in Charge* shows how to get started.'

Nic Turner, Head of Organisation Development, Boots the Chemists

'This is the first place I've ever worked where everybody acts like adults and does a very good job.'

Judy Nothern, US District Court, Western District of Washington

'Using participative design as an implementation approach to self-managing teams has unleashed encouraging enthusiasm for the pilot teams and their managers. It's early days yet, but I feel we are using an approach that will demonstrate long term business and individual value.'

Ros Bailey, Organisation Development Manager, Life & Pensions, Prudential

Contents

Introduction

Purpose of This Book

This book is a practical guide you can use to design your workplace to be self managing. It contains the concepts, do-it-yourself guides, and case examples you need to get you started on the road to self management. The basic premise of this approach is that organisation effectiveness – quality products and services – results when you redesign your workplace to be self managing. And, that the people who do the work are the ones who know best how to redesign it. Self managing workplace design is a participative way to get everyone in your organisation involved in workplace effectiveness.

People In Charge is for you if your organisation is considering workplace redesign. Any kind of organisation – corporation, small business, public sector, or government agency – can become more productive and effective by changing its structure to self management. The book is for managers who are considering the benefits of changing to self management, and what steps they can take to make sure real change happens. Workers will find this book a useful guide for understanding how self management can provide them more satisfaction at work, and at the same time make the organisation more successful. The book is also a resource for consultants and trainers wanting to learn effective ways for implementing self management.

Acknowledgements

The idea for a practical book on designing self managing workplaces sprung from the Fifth European Ecology of Work Conference in 1997 in Dublin. It was at the afternoon tea break one day during the conference that several of us planned this book and promised to make it happen. The tea drinkers were Phil Glaser and Steve Hobbs from South Africa, Nancy Cebula and Kevin Purcell from the USA, Australians Peter Aughton and Bob Baxter, and Martin Large of the UK. They, and others from around the world, have contributed to the writing of this book.

The Ecology of Work Conference co-ordinators were Tom Chase of the USA, and Kevin O'Kelly and Eberhard Köhler of the European Foundation for the Improvement of Living and Working Conditions. Thanks to them for their dedication to spreading the news around the world about workplace innovations.

Along the way, I also began writing about Kurt Lewin and Fred Emery, two pioneers of workplace democracy. I wanted the world to remember the contributions of Kurt Lewin some fifty years following his death in 1947. The words and ideas of Lewin are here, spread around the book. Kurt Lewin was a social psychologist and Jew who escaped Nazi Germany in the mid 1930s. His direct experience of the horror of autocracy led him to a life long study of the potential of democracy – in society, communities, and workplaces. Lewin invented group dynamics, action research, and the field we now call organisation development. People call Kurt Lewin the practical theorist because he considered theory and practice inseparable.

Fred Emery took the seeds of self management planted by Kurt Lewin and made them sprout. He turned Lewin's ideas about democratic and autocratic leadership into workplace design principles. Along with his colleague Eric Trist and others, Emery invented socio-technical systems as a practical way of redesigning work in the British coal mines in the early 1950s. Then he applied socio-technical analysis tools in the Norwegian workplace democracy projects in the 1960s. Emery's biggest contribution is the participative design workshop, a practical and conceptually sound method for redesigning a workplace to be self managing. Emery, too, was a practical theorist. You will find quotations and insights from both Fred Emery and Kurt Lewin throughout the book.

Special thanks goes to Merrelyn Emery who encouraged me several years ago to write an adaptation of her writings on participative design. And thanks to Rod Muth, Tom Devane, Chris Hoffman, and Gary Frank for their support and feedback during various stages of the writing.

Overview of the Book

The first four chapters of the book provide a foundation for understanding what we mean by self managing workplace design. Chapter 1 describes the design principle of self management in detail. Chapter 2 makes the link between organisation design and human productivity. Chapter 3 gives some background on the historical development of self management earlier in this century. And the fourth chapter emphasises the importance of participation in the design of any workplace.

Chapters 5 through 8 provide practical information on how to redesign your workplace to be self managing. Chapter 5 is a detailed discussion of the participative design workshop, an effective method for designing a self managing workplace. Chapter 6 is the story of how the Land Bank of South Africa used participative design workshops to redesign their branch banks to be self managing. The Land Bank gives a real life example of how the workshop can fundamentally change an organisation from bureaucratic to self managing. Chapter 7 goes into detail spelling out what an organisation should do to get ready for the change to self management. And Chapter 8 is a practical guide new teams can use to get started on the path to self management.

The next seven chapters are real life case examples of organisations that have changed to self management. The first case, Chapter 9, is the story of how Prudential Assurance

Company of the UK used the participative design workshop to redesign its call centre, putting workers in control of their own technology and customer service. Chapter 10 is the story of the Australian wine maker, Southcorp, who found it more profitable and productive to redesign its biggest wine making facility to a self managing team structure. Chapters 11 and 12 are about the U.S. Court system's process for redesigning its district and bankruptcy court operations, and probation departments to a team based structure. Orchestrating Success, Chapter 13, is the remarkable story of how the Orpheus Chamber Orchestra took up self management to produce beautiful music that brings down the house performance after performance. Chapter 14 tells how the Do It All stores are using self managing teams to bring customer service to their customers.

Chapter 15 is about macro organisation design, the marketplace alignment imperative. If the principle for workplace design is putting workers in control of their workplace, this chapter answers the question of how to design at the enterprise or corporate level, involving the redesign of multiple functions across an organisation of perhaps thousands of workers.

The book closes with stories from workplace redesign experiences – Chapter 16. In a series of short vignettes, the compelling reasons for changing to self management become clear. Putting people in charge of their workplace means transformation for the workers, mangagers and ultimately, the whole organisation.

Why Change to Self management?

Things are changing everywhere, and we all know it. The world has become increasingly uncertain and turbulent in recent years. The world is changing so fast that our social institutions, particularly workplaces, are struggling to keep up. Anyone born after 1960 has never experienced a time when social conditions were more stable than now. Fred Emery and his colleague Eric Trist coined the term 'turbulent environment' one day in the early 1960s after a bumpy airplane flight. Taking their cue from the troubled sky, they predicted that turbulence would accelerate in the world, spinning us into more and more uncertainty. They thought the results for society would be: breakdown in community life; a general deterioration of co-operative ways; and a more competitive, alienating, and lonely cultural environment.

Emery and Trist considered self management a practical way for coming to terms with the turbulent world. Human events caused global turbulence; humans can change it. The place for change is the workplace, they thought, because that's where people spend so much of their time. Through self management, people can build local workplace communities where they have a more successful relationship with their surrounding world. As workplaces build self managing work communities, workers begin reducing the uncertainty and alienation they experience in their lives. The result is productivity in the workplace, and the community, too.

Some time ago, the top managers of a company with many retail stores met to explore the idea of changing to a team based organisation. The topic of their inquiry was: 'Why change to self management?' To start the discussion, I asked them what was changing in their surrounding business environment. The managers brainstormed all the changes in their environment affecting the future success of the company. Here's some of the changes they listed:

> Heightened competition in their industry; customer demand for better services and quality products; rapidly changing market conditions; increased government scrutiny; accelerating changes in communications and technology world wide; a global economy that is increasingly interdependent and unstable.

The list went on and on, covering several pages of chart paper. Next they talked about changes in their larger social environment. These included:

> Increased alienation among people; fragmentation of society; increasing evidence of a global shift to democratic forms of government; people looking for a deeper sense of community and belonging; increasing gap between the have's and have nots; and a general movement among people towards higher levels of education.

The managers discussed what all these changes meant to the company and its future. They decided their environment was sending them a strong message. The message was clear: the nature of their business and social environment was such that they could not be successful in it the way they were currently structured. Their business environment was becoming increasingly turbulent, demanding, and fast changing. In order to perform well in this turbulent environment, they needed an organisation design that was team based, that put decision making at the floor level, and a design that was full of highly skilled people who are customer driven.

- ♦ **Team based** because they needed a workplace in which workers cooperated and supported one another to meet the needs of their customers. Everyone should be focused on one thing working together to provide the best possible service to customers.

- ♦ **Decision making at the floor level** means people who do the work can make decisions on the spot reducing the usual customer run around.

- ♦ **Full of highly skilled people** who have broad and deep knowledge of the company's products and services and can move to whatever job needs doing.

- ♦ **Customer focused** because the retail industry is so competitive that customers will just go down the street if they can't get the service they want.

The team decided to move ahead with a plan to redesign their retail stores to self management. It was what they had to do to thrive in their turbulent environment. Perhaps this scenario is familiar to you. Maybe conditions look a bit different in your organisation's environment, but the basic elements no doubt appear when you scan the environment in which you are doing business.

People sometimes wonder why it has taken self management so long to take root in organisations around the world.
After all, the concepts have been around for fifty years. If self
management is such a good way to produce quality products
and services, why is it only becoming popular now? Maybe it's
just another management fad! The answer can be found in the
nature of our turbulent global environment. The more turbulence
becomes the way of the world, the more workplaces need to
respond by putting self management in place to face it.

For a long time we put our faith in bureaucratic social institutions with dominant hierarchies – military, government, church,
and workplace. The advent of the industrial revolution ushered
in the bureaucratic work organisation of command and control
that has become the model for corporations and all kinds of
organisations. This worked when our social environment was
simple, resources were cheap and abundant, and the labour
force was unskilled and uneducated. Now we need a new kind
of workplace that is effective in the twenty first century. These
new workplaces need to be created, maintained, and recreated
by the people who work in them.

So, what are we are changing to, anyway? Some people call
the new form of work organisation the 'high performing workplace'. Others use the term 'team based organisation' to describe
it. Yet other people prefer to just say 'self directed teams' or 'self
directed work groups'. The original words used in the early
British coal mining studies were 'semi-autonomous groups,'
but that proved to be a mouthful. Some people dare to use the
word 'democratic' when talking about this new form of
workplace. Other team terms come to mind – empowered, self
regulating, and self managing. You will see some these terms
used in the cases in this book. They are all good ways to
describe what's happening in today's workplace.

The point is that changing to a new form of workplace
means changing the structure of the workplace so workers can
take responsibility for producing high quality products and
services. In this book, I call it changing the structure of your
organisation to a self managing workplace.

Chapter 1
The Self Managing Workplace

Let's start by saying what we mean and don't mean when we use the term 'self managing workplaces.' Self managing workplaces *are* organisations where people are responsible for controlling and coordinating their own work. They *are* workplaces where people share responsibility and have freedom to make decisions about their work. They are places where managers and workers negotiate and influence one another towards the accomplishment of shared goals. Self managing workplaces *are* organisations where everyone is riveted on producing the highest quality product or service for customer or client.

Self managing workplaces are *not* ordinarily organisations where workers get to determine what product to make or what service to provide. They are *not* workplaces where workers vote for their managers, nor are they organisations that use representative means to run their business. Self managing workplaces are *not* chaotic, unstable, or unstructured. They are *not* laissez faire, *not* everyone for themselves, *not* anything goes. They are *not* workplaces where people do whatever they want. Nor are they master servant, superior subordinate, or dominant submissive.

I coined the following definition of an organisation one day after seeing yet another example of an ineffective workplace design: *An organisation is a collection of ordinarily nice people doing terrible things to one another with good intentions.'*

You know the story. It happens every day in workplaces, whether corporate or public sector. There's no shortage of good people in any of our organisations. But when you ask people what gets in the way of their doing their best work, they frequently report how their co-workers are busy stabbing them in the back, and how the boss is mistreating them. Perfectly nice people walk in the workplace door in the morning and the backstabbing begins. It's not always this way, but it happens with enough regularity to make you wonder why. The problem isn't bad people, or even the need for better training in human relations. The problem is that too many workplaces are designed to get the worst out of people.

If you want your workplace to be self managing, you can design it that way. It doesn't matter what kind of organisation you are. Any workplace – private company, hospital, N.G.O., school, or government agency – can change to self management. It's a matter of choice!

The Choice of Design Principles

There are two principles[1] that describe different choices for designing a workplace. These two principles are not rigid rules, but more like the genetic code, or the seeds, from which an organisation can grow and develop. The two principles describe very different ways of structuring an organisation.

When we use the word 'structure' we are talking about the patterns of relationships among people, tasks, and responsibility at all levels of the organisation. Structure is about who does what work, with whom, and how that work is controlled and coordinated. Designing an organisation's structure is all about getting people organised around the work so that they can do quality work and have worthwhile jobs.

The first design principle: *Locate responsibility for control and coordination of work at least one level above where the work occurs.*

We call organisations designed according to this principle bureaucratic workplaces. The structure of this kind of workplace is bureaucratic. This is a workplace in which workers are like cogs in a machine. The diagram describes the bureaucratic workplace.

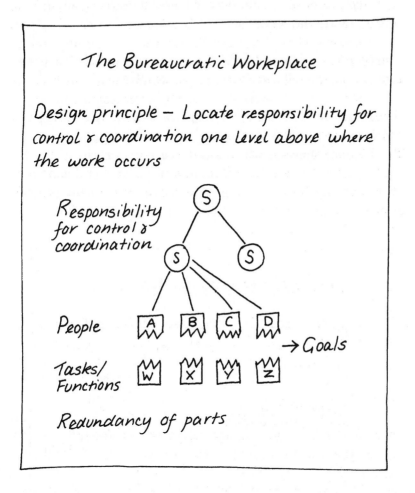

The basic building block of this type of organisation is one person (let's call that person 'A'), one job (X), watched over by a supervisor (S). The supervisor is responsible for control and coordination of the work below. It's the supervisor's job to decide what each person (A, B, C, D) will do regarding the tasks (X, Y, Z, W) assigned to them. Person A is limited to doing task X, and is not permitted to do tasks W, Y, or Z. Often task

X is a segmented, limited bit of work. The supervisor is responsible for the goals and performance of the workers. People in the bureaucratic workplace spend much of their work time in a state of dependency, looking up to see where the supervisor is, what the supervisor wants, how to please the supervisor, or how to get around the supervisor.

The second design principle: *Locate responsibility for the control and coordination of work with the people who do the work.*

The structure of this kind of workplace is democratic. The basic building block of this workplace is the self managing group. As the diagram shows, a self managing group consists of people (ABCD) responsible for shared control and coordination of their work (WXYZ) towards the achievement of the group's goals.

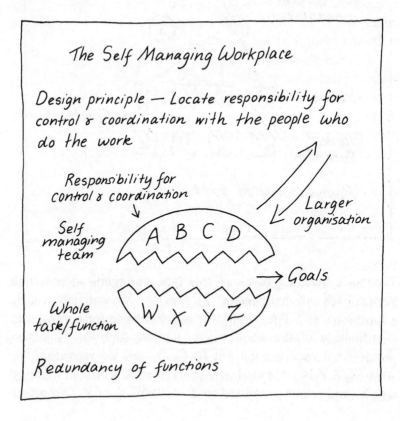

The Self Managing Workplace

Design principle — Locate responsibility for control & coordination with the people who do the work

Responsibility for control & coordination

Self managing team

Larger organisation

A B C D

→ Goals

Whole task/function

W X Y Z

Redundancy of functions

People in a self managing group normally do not have job descriptions; the group has work to do. Group members have the skills that make it possible for them to move to whatever work needs doing. The group shares the task of controlling the contributions of its own members. Responsibility and accountability belong to the work group.

We use the word 'redundancy' when describing the design principles. Organisations need to contain a certain amount of redundancy if they are going to be flexible and adaptive. Here, the word redundancy is used the way engineers use it. Engineers build redundancy, or back up, into a system so it can cope with varying demands. Every system needs some allowance for duplication so that a system does not fail because of the breakdown of a single part. When you ride in a B747 jet, you want to know that all the important technical systems, such as instruments and computers, are backed up, that they are redundant. In workplace design, there are two ways to build redundancy into an organisation – redundancy of parts and redundancy of functions.

The bureaucratic workplace is redundancy of parts because each person is treated like a replaceable part. When one part (person) fails, another is put in its place. An example is the traditional assembly line where a worker is limited to a segmented bit of work, and can be easily replaced by another worker who needs little, if any, training to do the simple tasks. Bureaucratic design is not limited to factory work. Workplaces of all kinds are designed to devalue and deskill workers. In today's information age, you can see redundancy of parts in many service centres. People work in modern 'sweat shops' answering phone calls or operating machines, all the while being monitored by electronic means out of their control.

The self managing workplace is redundancy of functions because in the self managing group many people can perform a variety of tasks. By adding functions to the parts (people), each person is able to perform many functions, and, therefore, contribute to the success of the organisation. Examples are: self managing teams of factory workers who are multi-skilled; teams of service representatives; cross functional professional teams responsible for research and development; marketing and sales teams with joint responsibility for customer satisfaction; teams of people with mixed skills working on the oil pipeline solving problems together. No matter what the work – labour or knowledge oriented – redundancy of functions can be designed into that work.

The choice of design principles is not a battle between good and bad. The choice marks a shift from a bureaucratic design that worked in more stable, predictable times to a design that is suitable for today's turbulent, uncertain world. The choice of design principles is not the only way to change an organisation, but it is the way that will unlock other changes to follow. Changing to self management is the lever that pulls everything else along with it – like communications, motivation, and commitment. The change to self management leads to productivity, quality, and a focus on customers and stakeholders.

Using Design Principles

Every workplace is based on one of the two design principles. The bureaucratic workplace is so prevalent that we often don't see design as a matter of choice at all. We automatically assume that bureaucratic design is the way to go. We forget that the design of any workplace is a human creation.

For any workplace design to be effective, the workers who live in it must sense that it is theirs, that they own it. Workers become committed when they design their own workplace in a participative process. It's the self managing structure (like a self managing team) that produces commitment, an interest in learning new skills, focusing on the customer, and all the rest. The relationship[2] looks like this:

Self managing Structure >> Commitment >> Productivity & Quality

When people design their workplace to have a democratic structure, they become committed to it. The results are higher productivity and quality. It's about changing design principles, changing the location of responsibility. Without using the design principles as your guide, you might be misled. You might think, as some experts claim, that process re-engineering or other technical changes will lead to workplace productivity. Or you might think that human relations training and team building will do the trick. Or maybe cross training alone without a self managing group structure is the key. Using design principles, on the other hand, is a structural approach to workplace design.

For any design principle to be useful, it must be simple and deep. Principles, to be worthwhile, need to be simple to understand and at the same time be a deep reflection of the human experience. Humans have lived in democratic structures for almost all of their existence over thousands of years. We have only lived and worked in bureaucratic structures in modern times. Using the design principle that locates responsibility for control and coordination where the work occurs, is easy to grasp and natural to apply. It is human!

Characteristics of Self Managing Workplaces

Self managing workplaces are organisations based on the design principle that says, 'Locate responsibility for control and coordination of work with the people who do the work.' Every self managing workplace is unique, but they all share some common characteristics. If you were to walk into a self managing workplace tomorrow morning, these are some of the attributes you would see.

The self managing workplace is made up of self managing teams at all levels of the organisation – work groups, mid-management, and top management. It's truly a team based organisation. The relationship between management and work teams is not superior subordinate, or master servant. Management is not laissez faire or anything goes. In the self managing workplace, management is no longer responsible for the work of individual workers. Responsibility and accountability for the production and service work of the organisation resides with the work teams. Managers form themselves into self managing teams that are now responsible for their own work – providing strategy, coordinating across functions, and negotiating goals with self managing groups.

To be self managing, people need to know that membership of their group is mostly under their control. They are free to organise their own leadership and internal group structure. Leadership and training roles rotate around the group as needed. The group decides how to allocate work and manage on the job training. It's the responsibility of the group to improve its own functioning and skill.

Typically, self managing teams are responsible for: assigning members to daily tasks; managing their own sick leave and holiday schedules; handling new hiring, training, and disciplining of members; coordinating supplies; working with customers and stakeholders; and coordinating their team's efforts with the larger organisation.

In the self managing workplace, groups set their own group production and development goals that are comprehensive, clear, realistic, and challenging. And they get feedback about their group's performance. It is a workplace in which management and workers negotiate goals. The negotiations between management and work groups can be tough and challenging, and are characterised by respect and directness.

Groups in self managing workplaces are self managing, but not autonomous. They work hand in hand with other groups, management, and customers to get the job done. They use equipment belonging to the larger organisation. They rely on the larger organisation for strategy, human resource policies, and attention to regulatory concerns.

Self managing work groups maintain open, clear documentation of goals, methods, and responsibilities. When you walk into a self managing workplace, you see charts on the walls documenting progress on team goals such as production, safety, and training. In the self managing workplace, information flows throughout the organisation.

Workers on self managing teams are compensated for their skill and knowledge. The multi-skilled work group is composed of people who possess a variety of skills needed by the team so it can do its work properly. Teams typically manage their own pay systems through skill testing and review. Self managing workplaces use organisation-wide and group based bonus systems to reward people for co-operative working and productivity gains.

The position of supervisor is not part of the structure of the self managing workplace. In the self managing workplace, supervisors frequently become work group members or organise themselves into a self managing group responsible for providing technical resources to the organisation.

The level of self management that an organisation takes on varies widely and depends on the nature and circumstances of the organisation. At the early stages of self management, teams may take responsibility for allocating work among members, but not discipline. At higher levels of self management, teams may be actively involved in strategic planning and may control team budgets. It's up to the organisation to determine what self management means for them.

The Design of Managerial Work

So what happens to management in the self managing workplace? The diagram for the design principle of self management shows only the work group as the building block of the organisation. The reason is that the work group, whether their work is making a product or providing management, is the basic design choice. In reality, large organisations have many work groups. Here is a real example of a workplace designed along the lines of the self management. The organisation is the federal bankruptcy court operation located in a large American city.

People

In

Charge

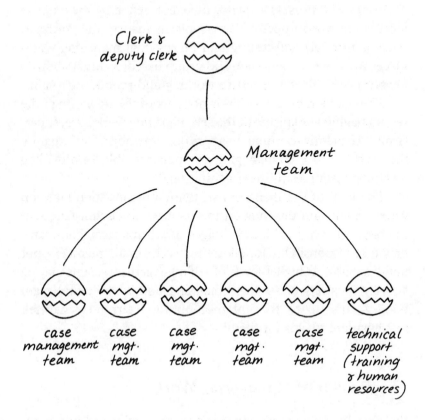

The old bureaucratic design had people organised according to function. For example, there was a filing section in the old organisation with each employee in it reporting to a filing supervisor, who in turn reported to a middle manager in charge of documentation. In the new design, the workplace is made up of several self managing teams, each one multi-skilled to perform an entire beginning to end function for the court and its clients, all the way from intake to filing. The teams split the workload up according to the alphabet. Team A is responsible for client cases from letters 'A' to 'K.' And so on for the other teams. Some of the ex-supervisors organised themselves into a service team responsible for training, human resources, and information technology. The three middle managers coordinate the overall office workload. The chief and deputy clerk attend to the external environment of the court office, developing their working relationships with the judges and the Administrative Office of the U.S. Supreme Court.

As this example shows, workplace design does not stop at the 'shop floor.' Management also redesigns itself to be self managing. There is no dominant hierarchy in a self managing workplace, but the structure may still have levels such as management and work groups. The difference is in the relationships up, down, and across the organisation. In the self managing workplace, the relationships are transactional, not master servant. By transactional we mean that management and work groups negotiate (transact) goals with each other, each respecting the other's knowledge and experience.

Barry Oshry has written with clarity about the system dynamics of middle management in organisations. His ideas about the middle help us see how to design middle work. In the bureaucratic workplace, middle management is a crunching, tearing place. Middles find themselves crunched in-between top and bottom issues. Or they get caught in conflicts across the functions of the organisation. They react by sliding into the middle of other people's problems and making them their own. Or they just check out. How often have you heard top management and workers blame the middle as the real cause of the organisation's problems? They are called the wall, the roadblock to communication, or the concrete in the system. In the middle, it's every person for him or herself. Team work is rare among middles. They are dispersed from one another – alienated. In bureaucratic organisations, middles are expected to keep their area in line, to watch over workers who cannot be trusted on their own. Structurally, middles are set up to compete with one another. This is a shame, because workplaces need strong middles to coordinate the overall operations of the system. Middle work is important.

In the self managing workplace, 'Middles of the world, integrate!' Middles have the opportunity to be the integrators of the workplace, working together as a strong middle group. Being integrators means sharing information and solving problems across functional boundaries. Integration involves planning and strategising for the organisation.

In an organisation we know, the five middle managers redesigned themselves to be a self managing team. It was a manufacturing plant. The old design had middle managers heading up functional sections such as assembly, engineering, production control, testing, and maintenance. The middle managers rarely cooperated across their boundaries. Instead they competed with one another for the attention of the top manager. The workforce had already completed their own workplace design process and had reorganised themselves into self managing teams. Supervisors either joined work groups or became part of a new technical support group.

The middle managers designed themselves to be a middle group responsible for the overall operation of the plant. They took responsibility for the following work: setting production goals for the plant; monitoring the plant's performance; co-ordinating plant wide information flow; resolving problems across functional boundaries such as engineering and assembly; negotiating goals with work teams, challenging them towards higher levels of performance.

This new design of middle work gave the middle manage-ment team an important and energising role in the wider organisation. It also allowed work groups to become fully self managing because they were clearly responsible for their own production work. Top management also benefited from the middle managers' new design. Tops were free from day to day concerns, turning their attention to the organisation's business environment and long term strategy. Integrating the middle paid off for the whole workplace.[3]

Self managing workplaces are organisation designs in which people – workers and managers alike – are responsible for their own work. The workplace is structured for people to do quality work to be productive members of the organisation who deliver the best possible products and services to customers and clients.

Chapter 2

Doing Productive Work – Six Criteria for Productive Work

Being productive is a basic human need. Kurt Lewin said, 'People don't live to produce, they produce to live.' We have a psychological (and probably biological) need to be productive; it's a natural part of being human. Being productive means being creative, caring about quality in whatever we are doing, and being useful.

Bureaucratic workplaces are structured to prevent people from satisfying their human need to be productive. Doing quality work comes naturally to people when their environment is structured for it to blossom. You can design your workplace to unleash people's natural tendencies to learn and perform, to be productive. The self managing workplace is an environment in which people can have an impact and be useful.

Here's a thought[1] from the American biologist Lewis Thomas:

> 'One human trait, urging us on by our nature, is the drive to be useful, perhaps the most fundamental of all our biological necessities. We make mistakes with it, get it wrong, confuse it with self regard, even try to fake it, but it is there in our genes, needing only a better set of definitions for usefulness than we have yet agreed upon.'

Fred Emery and Einar Thorsrud identified six human needs that should be satisfied for people to do productive work. They are called the six criteria for productive work. We use these six human needs when designing a self managing workplace. In order for an organisation to be effective and deliver quality products and services, it has to be designed to satisfy these human needs.

1. Elbow room for decision making. To be productive, we humans need enough freedom of movement in order to feel that we can control our own efforts. At the same time, we need enough direction to know what to do. Each person has his or her own optimal level of elbow room. One person may thrive on lots of freedom, while another, doing the same job, prefers less involvement in decision making. Almost everyone, though, does not appreciate a boss hovering over them, breathing down their neck, telling them what to do. To some extent, people need to feel as if they are their own boss.

The bureaucratic workplace is traditionally a place where every person has someone higher up, like a supervisor, who is responsible for making decisions about their work. Each level of the hierarchy is there to watch over the work of the next lower level. Now we even see electronic surveillance used to make sure people do their work. The basic assumption of the bureaucratic workplace is that people are unreliable by nature, and need watching over, or they won't perform properly.

In the self managing workplace, workers share responsibility for team decision making about work they are responsible for doing. In a self managing team, each person is aware of the needs of fellow members relating to elbow room. Teams become sensitive to the fact that one member needs more room than another for doing their own work, while others may need more direction. Everybody needs their own level of control over what they do.

2. Ongoing learning. There's much discussion these days about the learning organisation and how to get one. The truth is that people are learning all the time. Being alive is a process of constant learning. The problem is that the bureaucratic workplace inhibits learning on the job.

Learning in this view is the ability to set goals and get feedback. People learn when they set reasonably challenging goals for themselves, and then make sure they get timely, accurate feedback to see how they did. The combination of goal setting and feedback is what we call learning. Take golf as an example. Almost everyone who plays golf, from the pro Jack Nicklaus to a duffer like me, is constantly trying to improve their game. Your goals may be quite simple – to shave five strokes off your score, or maybe for some of us, not to lose any more golf balls. When you hit the ball, feedback comes immediately. You see the ball go into the rough, your playing partner says – 'too bad!' – again, and you feel that awful sensation of mishitting a driver. Your friends then give you some helpful advice on improving your swing and you try again.

Learning on the job is similar. The difference in the bureaucratic workplace is that usually goals are set somewhere else, by someone up there. The goals may not be realistic or achievable, or maybe not challenging enough. Feedback is often a surprise when you didn't know you had a goal to begin with. Feedback from customers may come filtered through several levels of management, making it not very specific, and certainly long after the work was done. In the self managing workplace, to the extent possible, teams set their production and service goals, as well as skill development goals. Teams manage their own feedback processes, putting in place mechanisms, surveys, checkpoints all along the production or service delivery process.

3. Variety. Every person has their own need for variety. Getting the right level of variety is a balancing act between boredom and fatigue. Being productive means being able to vary your work tasks so you don't get too bored or too over stimulated. Bureaucratic workplaces are typically variety decreasing places. Jobs are designed to prevent people from using all their skills and talents. Job descriptions can be strait jackets keeping people in their proper place. Cross training may be allowed in some bureaucratic workplaces, but seldom are workers encouraged to learn management skills.

A well designed self managing workplace offers opportunities for everyone to optimise their needs for variety. If a team is designed to be multi-skilled, people can get training on new technical tasks. There are no job descriptions in the self managing workplace, just work groups with a variety of work to do. The opportunity to vary your work in a self managing workplace extends to what used to be supervisory or management work in the old design. Leadership and management work rotate around the team, giving everyone a chance to do new things.

4. Mutual support and respect. The golden rule is to treat people as you would have them treat you. It's natural for people to cooperate and help one another. Humans need to cooperate, to work together towards a common goal. Bureaucratic workplaces are set up to discourage co-operation and to encourage competition among workers. In some cases, people don't help one another at work because they don't have the skills to do so, or it's not part of their job, not in the job description. In other cases, people in the bureaucratic workplace don't provide support because they don't want anyone else to look good (but them) in the eyes of the boss.

In a workplace with self managing teams, people have the skills to do all the work of the team. They can jump in and give a helping hand if needed. It's also in everyone's interests to give mutual support on a team, because we're all in it together. The structure of self managing teams encourages mutual support and the respect that goes with it. Getting the right amount of support and respect in the workplace knows no bounds. You can never have too much.

5. Meaningfulness. We all know that what separates humans from other life forms is the need to find meaning in all that we do. In the workplace, people need to feel that they are having an impact because of the work they do. They need to feel some connection between what they do all day and some higher benefit to their community, or society at large. Bureaucratic workplaces limit workers to just doing their often disconnected bit of work. It's only upper management that appreciates the value the product or service has to customers and users. The very make up of jobs in the bureaucratic workplace is such that people do not see the whole product, beginning to end.

I once toured a hi-tech manufacturing plant. The plant had a traditional assembly line. At the end of the line was the testing area. The product looked to the outsider like big electronic boxes. So I asked one of the test technicians to tell me about his job. He seemed to appreciate my interest. He showed me how he monitored the testing measurement equipment to make sure the product worked properly. I asked him a question, 'What is this product used for?' 'I dunno,' he said with embarrassment. 'I just test 'em.' The technician's job did not include information about customers or the basic purpose of the product. No wonder quality was not happening in this company.

People can design their own workplace so that their teams are much like business units. Business units are riveted on customer satisfaction. They have the skills to make a whole product, or deliver a complete service. They are knowledgeable about everything from financial performance to customer requirements.

6. Desirable future. People thrive on hope for the future. They want things to be better tomorrow than they are today. Bureaucratic workplaces offer a dead end to most workers. Jobs are narrowly defined. Promotion is available for the few who measure up to management's expectations. In the self managing workplace, people typically report that they have a team environment in which they can learn and keep on learning. Training and development increase dramatically in this kind of organisation. Workers feel they have more influence over the success of the entire organisation. Instead of looking up for promotion, people look outward to the possibility of expanding their skills and earnings.

These six human needs are common across cultures and peoples throughout the world. These needs are in direct conflict with the structure of the bureaucratic workplace. In the bureaucratic workplace, people are deskilled and devalued by the very structure they work within every day. When people design their workplace to be self managing, they are creating an organisation structure in which each and every person can satisfy their needs to be a productive person. The goal in self managing workplace design is for people to design their work so that, as much as possible, each person can satisfy their human needs in the workplace.

Variety Increasing

When I was first trying to understand redundancy of functions, I asked Fred Emery, who came up with the principle, for a definition. 'What is redundancy of functions, anyway?' His answer, 'Variety increasing!' The answer sounded mystical until he explained it. Variety is increasing when people have an open horizon of personal development. Variety is increasing when they have the opportunity to learn and keep on learning when they can satisfy their needs for the right amount of challenge and routine. Variety is increasing when they can increase both their work skills and their room for decision making. Bureaucratic workplaces deskill and devalue people. The self managing workplace is a place where variety is not the spice of life, but the meat and potatoes. Variety is basic.

From a design point of view, once a work group structures itself to take responsibility for its own work, then the group will almost certainly become variety increasing. The group will begin multi-skilling to make sure it can achieve its production and quality goals, meeting the needs of its environment. In a self managing group, multi-skilling means the group can cover all the work that needs doing. Multi-skilling includes training in the technical work skills and functions required to get the group's work done. It also means that the group needs to get thoroughly educated about the larger organisational strategies, goals, products, and services.

The rule of thumb is that a group needs enough skills spread throughout the group to provide coverage. In some workplaces, the design may provide lots of multi-skilling to make sure that people can adaptively do whatever work needs doing. In other workplaces, particularly those with the need for specialist roles like doctors and scientists, the group design may have individuals with specialised roles. Even this kind of design requires overlapping knowledge and joint coordination of group goals.

Work groups need to have direct knowledge of their external environment. They need to be in regular contact with customers, suppliers, and other important stakeholders. They need to have mechanisms for regularly scanning their environment so they know what's happening around them. In a fast changing, turbulent world, an organisation needs to have the capacity to respond quickly. It has to possess an array of strategies, skills, and knowledge to deal with unexpected challenges and opportunities.

The Mystery of the Faulty Glue

This story[2] brings to life Fred Emery's insights about 'variety increasing' workplaces. Here's the scene: a warehouse floor strewn with a hundred computer storage units returned by dissatisfied customers because they didn't work properly. Managers are looking out over this scene, scratching their heads and wondering what could have gone wrong. Now the problem was to disassemble each product and make it over again from scratch. Each unit is worth thousands of dollars. Reworking them will bring the plant to a standstill.

The plant is a division of a larger company that manufactures hi-tech storage devices. The head disk assembly is one of their products that works something like the common disk player at home. The difference is that one unit can record and play back enormous amounts of information and is used by banks, airlines, and all kinds of other large organisations that have massive information storage needs.

After considerable soul searching, management decided that maybe the problem was in the design of the workplace, not the product. The plant was made up of managers, supervisors, operators who assembled the product, and engineers who over-saw the technical system. Most of the manufacturing process occurred in surgery-like clean rooms where the product was moved on a kind of assembly line from clean room to clean room. Each operator stood at a station and did the work of attaching, torquing, or gluing parts. The operators had no idea what the product was used for. They just did their bit and sent it down the line. If a problem occurred, it was too much trouble to call in the dreaded supervisor or consult the arrogant engineer. It just wasn't worth the trouble.

Everyone in the plant participated in redesigning their workplace to be self managing. Now the operators worked in self managing groups that controlled the production schedule and coordinated quality issues. Each operator now made his or her own products. The new work process called for each operator to assemble a whole unit, moving with the product along the assembly process, from room to room. They also formed special process teams made up of operators, managers, and engineers to manage process improvements and solve technical problems right away.

It didn't take long for the new design to uncover the source of the defect. Operators started talking to one another in the break room one day. Before, they had talked mostly about their hobbies at home, or the latest antics of the supervisor. Now they talked about the products they were making. One of them mentioned, 'You know, the glue I am using to make the connectors stick to the coils – when I get down farther in the process, it's just not sticking like it should.' Another operator chimed in, 'I noticed the same thing.' A third person said, 'Maybe there's something wrong with that glue, anyway.' The operator who had been there the longest remembered, 'It was three or four years ago we had the same problem. Back then the problem had to do with how much glue we scraped off.' So, they called together their cross functional process improvement group of engineers, operators, and managers to discuss what they had discovered.

As it turned out, the problem was not the glue but the procedures operators were using to apply it. It didn't take long for the operators to train each other in proper glue application. Within the first three months of implementation, quality improved 500% and the plant went on to win the company's quality award. What made the difference? One operator put it this way:

> 'Before we became responsible for "owning" our own products, I didn't care what happened to my work when it went downstream to another operator. Now there's no "them" down there anymore. It's all up to me because my name is on the product.'

Chapter 2
Doing
Productive Work
– Six Criteria for
Productive Work

Chapter 3

Where Did the Self Managing Workplace Come From?

The idea of the self managing workplace did not just fall off a passing truck yesterday. It has its roots in the development of workplace democracy over the course of this century. Two key landmarks on the road to self management were the leadership research of the 1930s and the British coal mining projects in the 1950s.

The Democracy Research of the Late 1930s

In the late 1930s, Kurt Lewin and his colleagues did research on leadership with boys from the Iowa Boys Club in the USA. This research is the source of our modern insights about designing workplaces. It's relevant today, now more than ever. The following is adapted from Kurt Lewin's report.

The researchers set up two kinds of experiments – autocratic and democratic. Along the way they discovered a third – laissez faire. In the autocratic approach, adult leaders told the boys what to do and how to do it. The adult leaders dominated the boys and judged their progress. The leaders started each activity with an order, then disrupted the order with new directions. They criticised the boys' work. As a result, the boys became either hostile or apathetic. They lost initiative, fought with each other, were aggressive, showed restless discontent, scapegoated other boys, damaged materials, and were concerned for themselves and not for the group.

When the adult leaders tried a different leadership approach, things changed. This time, goals and the means for reaching them were left to the group to determine democratically. At the beginning of each group activity, the leader and group discussed general steps to accomplishing the goal. Where technical advice was needed, the leader suggested alternatives from which a choice could be made. The boys were free to work with whomever they chose, and the division of tasks was left up to the group. The group was allowed a broader outlook. The researchers labelled this leadership democratic. Democratic groups were productive and friendly. They accomplished their task and showed group spirit doing it.

In laissez faire leadership, the third type, boys did whatever they wanted. They had complete freedom without any leader participation. As a result, their behaviour was less work centred; the boys were frightened, disturbed, and had less discussion. Scapegoating occurred in the laissez faire atmosphere, as it did in the autocratic. In laissez faire, scapegoating occurred because no leadership or ground rules existed. The feeling of inadequacy was lessened for some by ridiculing those who were less competent.

Kurt Lewin observed, 'On the whole I think there is ample proof that the difference in behaviour in autocratic and democratic situations is not a result of differences in the individuals. The group that had formerly been friendly, open, co-operative, and full of life, became within a short half hour a rather apathetic looking gathering without initiative.'

This early research proved that group effectiveness is more than leadership style or management behaviour. Productivity comes from the climate or conditions that are present in the workplace – now we call it the structure of the workplace. After almost sixty more years of continuing research and experience in organisations, we know that whether or not your workplace is democratic, autocratic, or laissez faire is a choice of design principles.

The lessons learned from the Boy's Club experiments were applied to the workplace by Lewin[1] and his students in 1939. Through Lewin's intervention, workers at Harwood Manufacturing Company's pajama plant in Virginia got involved in setting and monitoring their own production goals. Using group decision making and problem solving, the work group improved productivity, proving that self management and democratic work practices are an effective way to run a company. The Harwood experiments may be the first modern introduction of self management in industry. The rest, as they say, is history.[2]

Democracy: A Point on a Triangle, not a Stop along a Continuum

Conventional wisdom says that democracy, autocracy, and laissez faire are three management styles that exist on a continuum, and that managers move back and forth depending on circumstances. Kurt Lewin wrote about this common misunderstanding in 1945. His thoughts help clear up the confusion.

One way to define a form of group life is to compare it to others. Here we are comparing democracy, autocracy, and laissez faire (individualistic freedom). The usual way of depicting the three is on a continuum, putting autocracy on one end and laissez faire on the other end. In this picture, democracy is a moving target in the middle. It looks like this:

Autocracy «‹« *Democracy* »›» *Laissez faire*

People who think in terms of one continuum have no choice but to consider democracy something *between* autocratic discipline and lawlessness. On a continuum, democracy is a soft form of autocracy meant to induce group members to accept the leader's will. Today we call it buy in. It is important to dispel this myth if democratic living is to spread. The differences are not on a continuum but are points on a triangle. The diagram shows democracy, autocracy, and laissez faire as distinct points – completely different kinds of workplaces. The differences among the three types are deep. (Today we call them different paradigms.)

People
In
Charge

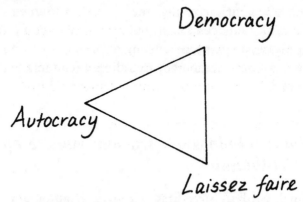

Autocracy – top down, hierarchical power relations; goal setting and policy making in the hands of the leader; workers responsible to the leader; not much individual freedom.

Democracy – horizontal interdependence of workers and work groups, with discussion and group decision making; goal setting in the hands of the group; the leader responsible to the group; individual freedom and responsibility.

Laissez faire – lack of interdependence; no group life, no goal setting, no leadership at any level.

'The superiority of democracy in creating fair minded and highly developed citizens is clear,' Lewin said. In the workplace, however, people have to meet production goals and deliver quality products and services on time. So, how does democracy affect efficiency in the workplace? Here's an example of how democracy is frequently misunderstood. Production goals in most workplaces are set and enforced by management with considerable pressure on workers to perform. Management, in an attempt to loosen control, decides to relax standards in the interest of morale. They think they are being more democratic by doing this. On the continuum shown above, democracy appears as a softening of autocracy. But loosening standards has nothing to do with democracy. Lowering standards in an autocratic workplace means a shift from the autocratic type to laissez faire, not a change to democracy. A shift to democracy involves shifting from imposed goals to goals set by work groups and negotiated with management.

You cannot create democracy by softening autocratic practices. Lewin said, 'An autocracy with a democratic front is still an autocracy.'

Democracy is a different type of workplace, not a stop between autocracy and laissez faire management.[3]

Self Management in the British Coal Mines: The Pub Research Story

Fred Emery told me this story of how he and his colleagues did research at the coal mines during the 1950s. It was this research project that led to the discovery of the self managing workplace. The setting is the coal mines of South Yorkshire, England. The story begins shortly after the end of World War II when England was busy rebuilding its industries. Coal mining was particularly important because of the need for cheap and efficient sources of power. Historically, coal mining was done by natural work groups made up of miners who could do the whole job from beginning to end. After the war, new forms of mechanisation were introduced to increase productivity, but the innovations failed to get the expected results. Mechanisation segmented work to the extent that the miners' jobs were broken down to a one man one task arrangement with close, coercive supervision. Productivity fell; absenteeism grew to 20%.

In one of the new seams, called Haighmoor, miners by themselves re-established the natural way of group working, with the support of management and the union. They interchanged jobs and shifts, providing most of their own supervision. The researchers called this new form of work 'semi-autonomous work groups,' and they began doing projects to spread the new workplace design to other coal mines in England.

There were two kinds of coal mining operations. One had semi-autonomous work groups; the other was the bureaucratic set up – segmented work closely supervised. Both operations were geographically close together – the same seam, neighbouring pits. The same cutting and hauling technology was in use. The bureaucratic group had 38 workers, split up into 14 groups, all doing separate work tasks, with separate pay. The semi-autonomous group had 41 all working together, rotating jobs, sharing a similar wage with group bonuses for productivity.

Emery and his colleagues did their research in local pubs. Anyone who knows English culture appreciates that the local pub is a centre of social life. The researchers found that doing interviews in the coal mines that had semi-autonomous work groups (now called self managing teams) was easy – and fun. All they had to do was go to the local pub. All the workers were there. These coal miners all mucked in together. At the pub, they were talking about the community, local sporting events, politics, and work. The workers were busy debriefing the day's events over pints of ale. Workplace and social life were united. The workers were productive and healthy.

Interviewing workers from the bureaucratic coal mines was another matter entirely. The researchers had to go to many different pubs. There was the pub where the cutters on day shift hung out after work. The scufflers also worked the day shift but the researchers found them in another pub complaining about the cutters and how they would get even with them the next day. The conversations in both pubs were tense, angry, and full of stress.

The fillers and hewers were on the next shift. As you might expect, the researchers split up to interview them in their respective pubs. Much of the talk of this shift was how the previous shift left unfinished work behind. The third shift had similar complaints – us against them. No one cared about anything but the work mates who shared the same job. The one thing all pub conversations had in common was a universal disregard for the bosses. There was much plotting for how they would pull the wool over the eyes of the boss. The bosses, of course, were deeply competitive with one another and did not even hang out together. Each went to a different pub. As you might suspect, the bureaucratic coal mine had productivity, sickness, and safety problems.

Fred Emery[4] came away from the coal mines realising that the workplace was the place to make change happen, the place to restore social life and associative community. The workplace is where people spend much of their waking hours and, historically, the workplace is the least democratic part of our social life. Emery considered the workplace the leading part of societal change. We have been doing our own version of pub research in recent years. The question is a simple one. 'How has the change to self management had an impact on your life?' These findings are typical: increased participation in community and social activities; improved communications in families and other relationships; less stress at home; more interest in being productive members of the community.[5]

Chapter 3
Where did the
Self Managing
Workplace
come from?

Chapter 4

Participating In Workplace Design

The way to build a self managing workplace is through participation. In practical terms, this means the people who do the work are the ones who redesign it. In self managing workplace design, everyone in the organisation joins together to redesign the organisation. It's a participative way to design.

Participation is the root of democratic life. When we use the word 'participative' in the context of workplace design, we are going beyond the way people often use the word. Participation is not 'buy-in'. It is not a technique for getting people to feel as though they are involved. Participation is not input to others, whether higher ups or representatives who actually make the decision. In bureaucratic organisations of all kinds, people's ideas are sent up the pipeline. Data are analysed up there and decisions are made up there. Usually, the information that went up comes back down looking mysterious to those who sent it up in the first place. People are told their ideas are important, but they often cannot see any connection between their ideas and the decisions coming back down. Frequently no connection exists. The usual result is cynicism. This is not what we mean by participation.

Many organisations are using what we call an autocratic approach to workplace redesign. These organisations try to move toward self management using autocratic, top down processes to get there. The desired outcomes are worthwhile –

less bureaucracy, decentralised structures, more empowered employees, and self directed work teams – but the process for getting there is anything but democratic. Simply changing from a centralised to decentralised operation may result in a leaner structure, but not necessarily self management. The recent re-engineering fad with its expert design teams and consultants is a too frequent example. The classic socio-technical systems design team approach also fits this scenario.

Not only is this kind of change process highly autocratic, so is the result. While the number of levels in the organisation is dramatically reduced, the autocratic management hierarchy is left in place. It only looks democratic on paper. While teams are implemented, often called self directed, these teams do not have responsibility for their own decision making. The few remaining managers keep the power to direct the work groups. Genuine self managing workplaces cannot be designed by force. People don't learn democracy this way.

An example of autocratic design is a semiconductor manufacturing organisation that wanted to install self directed work teams to increase productivity. The plant had about one hundred employees – managers, engineers, technicians and assemblers, and it was structured as a bureaucratic workplace. The plant manager decided that a flatter, team based structure would get better results. He hired an expert consultant to educate the workers about self directed teams. The consultant spent several days leading all the workers through a typical organisation design simulation, teaching everyone the benefits of team based design. At the end of the last workshop on Friday afternoon, the plant manager called all the workers and managers together to hear about his decision. The manager told everyone that starting Monday the plant would be organised into six self directed teams, each team assigned to a different part of the overall manufacturing process. He then publicly announced the names of workers assigned to each team. There was silence in the room; people were in shock.

On Monday, people reported to their new teams. They found immediately that the new design reduced their skill variety. Technicians and assemblers who were skilled across the entire process were now limited to the work of their new team. People also learned that their new teams had no increased level of responsibility for decision making. They were not self directed; middle managers took the roles of the old supervisors, keeping the autocratic hierarchy intact. The new team design never delivered the productivity hoped for by the manager. It was not long before the manager was replaced because of the poor performance of the plant and the teams were disbanded in favour of the traditional bureaucratic design. Shoving a pseudo-democratic design down the throats of workers is dangerous if you care about performance. People react by challenging management to walk its talk, seeing through the façade of democratic structure forcibly put in place.

Authentic participation has two defining elements. First, participation means being part of making decisions, and sharing responsibility for those decisions, because we made them together. Second, participation requires an environment in which people can have open, free conversation without threat of repercussions. Participation in workplace design means people are free to talk openly regardless of hierarchical position or status. So, true participation means people make free, open decisions about what is important to them and their work.

People build houses, make cabinets, work on their cars, invent new devices, write about their ideas, and dream about making a better world. People are designers by nature. We use the word design here to suggest that people can build workplace social structures as a matter of choice. Since the beginning of the industrial revolution and continuing with today's information age, the responsibility for design has been given to experts. Their design choice has been primarily bureaucratic, breaking work down into the smallest bits possible and taking decisions away from workers. This was done for purposes of control because people were not trusted to do what was expected. Experts design organisations as though they were machines with workers as cogs. But organisations are not machines; they are human systems.

Ordinary people are no longer accustomed to building and designing their own workplaces. It's like a muscle that has shrivelled from disuse. The natural capacity for design is there; it just needs to be exercised through participation and the knowledgeable use of design principles. The power to design is just waiting to be released. The only thing that can stand in their way as designers is an environment that prevents people from using their natural talents.

If you were designing a building, you would probably call in architects to design it, then contractors to do the building. Many approaches to organisation design are based on this kind of approach. It's as though human systems are a set of tinker toys that need to be fastened together. Expert organisation design consultants are hired. They apply the tools of their trade, often working alongside managers and design teams. When the design is finished, the experts leave and the organisation has a new structure that is perfectly designed – until they try to implement it with real people. Or until things change.

A different view is that people have the capacity to design their own workplaces. All they need is some basic knowledge of the choice of design principles and a learning environment in which they can collaboratively design their own work. Without the knowledge and experience of using design principles, people might end up with an organisation they could not sustain or change as times require. Designing a workplace is an ongoing, neverending story. No design is ever static; people are always changing and improving their designs over time.

Participation is important because of society's response to turbulent times. As our world wide environment has become increasingly turbulent and uncertain, people disconnect from one another. People react to the unpredictable nature of the environment we live in by retreating into their private lives. They keep to themselves, mind their own business, and withdraw from social responsibilities. We see this privatisation of life happening all around us as people look out for number one, hide behind suburban security systems, and stay glued to the television. The solution to disconnection is for people to associate in ways that produce real participation – shared decision making and the taking of joint responsibility. This perspective on participation is different from involving people

in sharing their ideas, or giving input, without being accountable for the outcome.

So, why is it important for workers to participate in the design
of their workplace? Here are the three key reasons:

♦ People who do the work know more about their own work
  than anyone;

♦ When people make their own changes, implementation is
  easier;

♦ When people make their own changes in a democratic
  learning environment, they learn participative ways of
  working.

It's true that people are more likely to implement a change they
make themselves. So one reason for participation is that it
makes implementation happen more smoothly. But there's an
even more important reason for having people participate in
designing their workplace. It's that workers are the best ones to
redesign their workplace because they know the most about
their own work. Not having workers participate in the
workplace design process runs the risk of producing a bad
design that is difficult to implement.

We use the participative design workshop to involve people
in redesigning their workplace to be self managing. The participative design workshop is designed to be a democratic, self
managing learning environment. When you use a democratic,
self managing learning environment to change an organisation's
structure, you are giving people an experience of working in a
self managing way.

Chapter 5

The Participative Design Workshop

The participative design workshop[1] is a practical way for people to design their workplace to be self managing. It is a tried and true method that people have been using around the world since 1974. The participative design workshop is appropriate for any kind of organisation – business, government, or not for profit. It works for people on the shop floor, professionals, research and development specialists, managers, and project teams – anywhere people need to organise themselves to get work done.

The purpose of the participative design workshop is to change the structure of a workplace from bureaucratic to democratic, putting people in control of their own work. People who use the method for redesigning their organisation become committed to implementing their own designs. They also learn the design principles that will guide them towards higher levels of self management over time.

The basic assumption underlying the participative design workshop is that the best designs come from the people who do the work being designed. Workers must 'own' their own section of the organisation if they are to do productive, quality work.

What follows is a description of the generic participative design workshop. Working from this general approach, you can craft the workshop to fit your organisation's unique circumstances. You can add analysis activities, or vary the following

activities to suit your needs. Remember, it's the principle –
locating responsibility with the people who do the work – that is
essential. As the American chef-philosopher, Julia Child, once
said, 'Good cooks don't follow recipes, they use principles.'

The typical participative design workshop occurs over two
days. The workshop has three phases. The first phase is an assessment of the current workplace design. Phase two is redesign of
the organisation's structure, and phase three covers all the practical matters that ensure that the new design will be effective.

Phase 1 – Assessment

Introduction. The workshop begins with introductions and a
detailed review of the agenda. None of this will come as a surprise
to participants, as they have already had full prebriefings before
the workshop begins. Nevertheless, this introduction is
important because it clarifies the purpose and activities of the
workshop. The agenda stays up on the wall, and is referred to
often, so everyone can see how the workshop is progressing.

PARTICIPATIVE DESIGN WORKSHOP

Assessment
Briefing: The Choice of Design Principles
Assessment: Six Criteria for Productive Work
Assessment: Skills

Redesign
Current Work Flow & Organisation Structure
Redesign structure to self management

Practicalities
Goals, training plan, control & coordination
processes, etc.

Briefing: The Choice of Design Principles – The Bureaucratic and Self Managing Workplaces. This briefing is a presentation of the two design principles the bureaucratic and self managing workplaces. The presentation points out how bureaucratic workplaces inherently fail to satisfy the six criteria for productive work, and how the self managing workplace does satisfy workers' needs to be productive. The presentation is simple and brief. (The content of this briefing is contained in chapters 1 and 2.)

Group Matrices for Six Criteria and Skills. People work in small design groups to assess their jobs as they exist today. They do this by completing two matrices: one an assessment of their jobs related to the six criteria for productive work; the other an assessment of skills they currently possess. These matrices show what human requirements and skills are lacking across the section or organisation being redesigned. People use this information later during the redesign phase.

People
In
Charge

6 Criteria for
Productive Work

1. Elbow room for
decision making

2. Ongoing learning

3. Variety

4. Mutual support
& respect

5. Meaningfulness

6. Desirable future

The Six Criteria for Productive Work

(See Chapter 2 for a more complete
discussion of the six criteria.)

1. Elbow Room for Decision Making. People need to feel that they are their own bosses and that, except in exceptional circumstances, they have room to make decisions they can call their own. On the other hand, they do not need so much elbow room that they just do not know what to do.

2. Opportunity to Learn On the Job and Go On Learning. Learning is a basic human need and activity. Learning is possible only when people are able to:
a) Set goals that are reasonable challenges for them, and
b) Get feedback of results in time for them to correct their behaviour.

3. Variety. People need to be able to vary their work to avoid the extremes of boredom and fatigue. They need to set up a satisfying rhythm of work that provides enough variety and a reasonable challenge.

4. Mutual Support and Respect. People need to be able to get help and respect from their co-workers.

5. Meaningfulness. People need to be able to relate what they do and what they produce to their social life. Meaningfulness includes both the worth and quality of a product, and having a knowledge of the whole product. Many jobs lack meaning because workers see only such a small part of the final product that its meaning is denied them.

Meaningfulness has two dimensions:
a) Socially useful, and
b) Seeing whole product

Taken together, these dimensions make it possible for a person to see a real connection between their daily work and the world.

6. A Desirable Future. Put simply, people need a job that leads to a desirable future for themselves, not a dead end. This desirable future is not necessarily a promotion, but a career path that will continue to allow personal growth and increase in skills.

Chapter 5
The Participative
Design
Workshop

The following examples describe the two matrices – *Six Criteria for Productive Work* and *Skills Held*. There is also an explanation of how the matrices are used in the participative design workshop.

The Six Criteria For Productive Work Matrix. The first task calls for the groups to complete the six criteria matrix (see the example matrix). The purpose of this assessment is to explore to what extent people are valued or devalued as human beings in the current organisation design. In open group discussion, people rate how much of each item they experience on the job currently.

Because the first three criteria need to be optimal for each individual, these three are scored from -5 (too little) to +5 (too much), with 0 being optimal, just right.

As the second three criteria are things you can never have too much of, they are scored from 0 (none) to 10 (lots).

The final group product will express the range of scores across the section. This activity normally takes about 45 minutes depending on the size of the group.

PSYCHOLOGICAL CRITERIA	NAMES OF PARTICIPANTS				
	NANCY	TOM	MARTIN	STEPHANIE	GARY
(1) Elbow Room	-3	0	-1	-3	-4
(2) Learning: (a) setting goals	-4	+3	-2	-3	-3
(b) getting feedback	-3	-4	0	-4	-4
(3) Variety	-3	+4	0	+3	-3
(4) Mutual Support & Respect	8	4	2	8	8
(5) Meaningfulness: (a) socially useful	9	9	8	9	7
(b) seeing whole product	4	10	7	3	4
(6) Desirable Future	3	8	5	2	2

The pattern in this example matrix is typical. Tom is the supervisor. He enjoys his autonomy but is overwhelmed with too many things to watch over. As supervisor he gets little feedback and respect. Nancy and Gary both have simple jobs. Stephanie probably gets stuck with the work. All three have low career paths and little potential on the job market. Nancy, Gary, and Stephanie stick together and look after each other. All recognise that the work of the group is socially useful, but only Jim and Martin really see how their bit contributes to the whole. This is an example of what people learn from this matrix.

A Note About Group vs. Individual Assessment

Practise what you preach when doing the assessment tasks in the workshop. This means being open and self managing in all that you do, particularly in the way people complete the six criteria assessment. In the participative design workshop, the six criteria assessment is a group task. Everyone in the group sits around the flip chart discussing their own scores as they see them. They share their perceptions of other's scores, discussing and negotiating differences in perceptions, changing their scores if necessary. Together they arrive at a collective picture of how their workplace presently meets their needs. This approach features openness, co-operation, and a sense that we are all in the same boat together.

The result is an assessment that will serve as an accurate basis for the design work that follows. People experience goodwill and humour that breaks down status barriers and makes it easy for people to participate. The group gets off to a good start. They learn about their workplace, about one another's jobs and how they see them, and about working participatively in a group. A cohesive group forms fast, as everyone is interested in talking about how their work is organised.

Skills Matrix. The second task for the groups to complete is a matrix of skills currently held. The purpose of this assessment is to determine to what extent the workplace is designed to skill or deskill workers.

First, people list all the essential skills required in the section being redesigned to make it work. Then, the groups compile a collective picture of their current skills by using a simple scale:

0 for none of a particular skill
One tick ✔ for a sufficient level of skill, or
Two ticks ✔✔ for high level of skill.

This activity can take an hour or more depending on the size of the group and the nature of the skills involved.

Example Matrix:

People
In
Charge

ESSENTIAL SKILLS	NANCY	TOM	MARTIN	STEPHANIE	GARY
A	✓✓	✓	0	0	0
B	✓	✓	✓	✓	✓✓
C	0	✓✓	✓✓	0	✓
D	✓	✓✓	✓✓	0	0
E	✓	✓✓	✓	0	✓
F, etc.					

The matrix shows that the section is covered at a high skill level only on skill C and D. If Nancy is sick, only Tom can cover for skill A at a lower level of skill, and he already has too much to do. The group can probably muddle through on skills B and E. The basic rule for a multi-skilled section is that there be at least two people with a high level of a particular skill with a back-up or two. In the discussion of this report, the group would mark skills A, B, and E as requiring more training. Later, in the practicalities session, they would return to this analysis and determine who should receive what training for which skills and whether it can be done on the job, and the time involved.

Phase 2 – Redesign

Redesign starts with two steps. First, groups draw their current work flow on chart paper. The purpose is for everyone to have a clear understanding of how work flows in the organisation being designed. The point is to focus on the overall understanding of the work of the organisation, not to dwell on every little step in the process. You are not changing or improving the process at this point, but better understanding it. The groups identify important decisions that occur in the process that are currently handled by supervisors.

Next, they draw their present organisational chart as it is today – real jobs, real people, formal organisational structure.

Now it is time to begin redesigning the structure of the organisation. The groups use the results of their assessment activities so that people can satisfy their human needs, the six criteria for productive work, and have the opportunity to learn new skills. The groups have the following information to work with:

♦ An assessment of the six criteria for productive work showing to what extent their workplace is currently structured to devalue the people working in it;

♦ An assessment of skills showing the extent to which the organisation's structure currently deskills people;

♦ An understanding of the work that flows through the organisation being redesigned;

♦ A diagram of the current organisation structure they are about to change.

In most cases, this is enough information for people to do good design work. Some organisations also provide information about the organisation's overall strategy and direction, as well as information about important customer and stakeholder expectations.

And, this is the time in the workshop to present and clarify any minimum critical specifications the organisation has that will guide the design process. These specifications may include policy and legal limitations, or areas that are not open to change in the design process.

Taking all this information into consideration, groups redesign their workplace to have a democratic, self managing structure. They draw circular diagrams similar to the diagram shown earlier describing the self managing workplace. They place the names of the members of the new self managing groups in the top part of the circles and list the work the groups are responsible for on the bottom. This activity can take about two to four hours to complete.

Groups present their designs and receive feedback and criticism from other groups. In cases where groups come from the same organisation, the various group designs need to be integrated into one final design.

Phase 3 – Practicalities

Briefing. This briefing describes the tasks that will ensure that new designs will work. It includes instructions for spelling out:

- ◆ Comprehensive and measurable goals for the groups. Goals include: quantity and quality of the team's product or service; team development goals, such as safety and social responsibility; and individual goals such as training. All these goals fit within the organisation's strategic plan. The goals are later negotiated with management;

- ◆ Requirements for training. This is a training plan including such specifics as who, how long, on or off the job, and to what levels;

- ◆ Arrangements for internal control and coordination, such as feedback mechanisms, processes for assuring job rotation, and regular meetings;

- ◆ Methods for coordinating external relations, such as maintaining relations with other groups and customers;

- ◆ Identification of equipment and resources needed for self management;

♦ A career path based on payment for proven skills held and skill blocks; this helps prepare the organisation for skill based pay;

♦ An explanation of how the design will improve their six criteria for productive work.

Groups complete their designs and get as far as they can with the practicalities tasks. Finishing these practicalities tasks in the workshop is not essential. It is important, however, that they get started on the tasks so that they can finish them later. It is useful if management is present to hear these, particularly if designs contain additional resource needs, changes to existing goals, or ideas about merging existing sections.

A few words are in order concerning the workability of certain designs. Watch out for designs coming out of the work-shop that do not change the structure from bureaucratic to self management, not really having people taking responsibility for control and coordination. For example, a group may go through the workshop and merely enlarge individual jobs without changing the location of responsibility. Or a group may improve its work processes without moving away from a bureaucratic structure. The participative design workshop is about structural change (people, tasks, and the location of responsibility), not process improvement. Once formed, self managing groups naturally begin improving their work processes because they feel ownership of their workplace. Job enlargement and process improvement are halfway measures that run the risk of inducing cynicism among the workforce, not productivity.

There are two other issues that are important to watch for in the workshop. The first issue concerns whether or not multi-skilling is appropriate as a design feature for your organisation. The second issue is what to do with the position of supervisor in the new self managing workplace.

To Multi-skill or not to Multi-skill

Multi-skilling is a common design feature of self managing groups. Multi-skilling means that people in the group can do a variety of tasks and functions. However, there are kinds of work where multi-skilling does not fit. Research and development organisations are examples of workplaces where multi-skilling is not appropriate. People in research and development organisations have diverse skills such as engineering, chemistry, or marketing. It is not right for a chemist to learn engineering skills. Multi-skilling makes no sense here, as each specialist cannot become an expert in all the team's disciplines.

Instead, people organise themselves into a self managing group that coordinates its tasks to assure the group meets its goals and delivers an effective product or service. In this kind of workplace, each person is responsible for their own work which is a specialised and whole piece of work. In project organisations with specialised skills, each person can control their own work, and now share responsibility with others for coordination of the project.

What About Supervisors?

The position of supervisor is not normally part of the structure of the self managing workplace. In the participative design workshop, supervisors can become work group members or they may organise themselves into a self managing team responsible for providing technical resources to the organisation. Either way, ex-supervisors are no longer responsible for the work of subordinates.

There is misunderstanding about what to do with supervisory positions. The conventional wisdom is that supervisors simply need to change their role to leader, coach, or facilitator. Supervisors are often told to change their roles and titles, but are still in the chain of command. They are responsible for the work product of *their* team. Or, as team leaders, coaches, or facilitators, they are responsible for the internal cohesion and functioning of *their* team. For example, they are often expected to continue doing performance reviews for *their* people. Regardless of what name or role is used for supervisors, if they are responsible for the team's output, they are in a master servant relationship with that team. Dominance can be experienced as autocratic control or human relations nurturance. Either way, people in the team become dependent on someone other than themselves. Self management does not develop in this kind of structure.

Shifting to an organisation design with teams led by ex-supervisors, no matter what they are called, is not a change to self management. Instead, it's a change from command and control to what I call a bureaucratic design with a human face. It's easy to determine if an organisation has implemented teams without changing the basic structure. The telltale sign is a structure with teams, sometimes called self directed, with one-time supervisors now in the new role of team facilitator, coach, or leader. The structure of the organisation is still bureaucratic. Responsibility for control and coordination of work remains with the supervisor, now called a coach, team facilitator, or leader. The dynamics of this structure look like this. Instead of focusing on goals and production targets, the team is side-tracked on its own relationships. Human relations, not production, becomes the paramount concern of the team. In addition, the team is confused about where their responsibilities start and end in relation to the ex-supervisor.

Increasing employee involvement by promoting better human relations – more openness, two way communications, facilitation – in a structure with unequal power can result in cynicism among workers because of the mixed message they perceive about power and authority. The key question to ask when designing is this. 'When there is a problem with a team's performance, who does management confront?' If the answer is the ex-supervisor who is now a trainer, leader, facilitator, or coach, the structure has not changed. Here's my favourite example of how one company shifted old supervisors to the new role of facilitator. They took the old job description of supervisor that had 10 task descriptions (all control oriented),

Chapter 5
The Participative
Design
Workshop

and added a number 11 – facilitate teams. They changed the supervisor's title, but kept the job intact.

A self managing group may decide to assign one of its members to be responsible for providing a coordinating function for the group on a rotating basis. For example, groups sometimes rotate the task of being contact person for the group so people have a consistent point of communication. Groups can provide for their own training, leadership, coaching, and facilitation. It's natural once a group accepts responsibility for its own control and coordination.

Designing Participative Design Workshops

Designing participative design workshops for your organisation is in itself a design art. The participative design workshop is flexible and adaptable, offering many variations in the way it is done.

The Design Team. Normally it is best to involve everyone in the workshops because it produces good designs and makes for easier implementation. If this is not possible, an alternative is to create a design team made up of a deep slice of the entire organisation. A deep slice means people from as many skills, functions, and levels as possible across the section. The actual choosing of the individuals according to these criteria can be done by the people in the section. The ratio of workers to supervisors and middle management should be kept as close as possible to the real life ratio. If a particular design team for a section is top heavy with supervisors and above, it is possible that the needs, ideas, and designs of the workers will not come through.

Again, the basic rule is the best designs come from the people who do the work. With the design team approach, not everyone can participate in the design workshops. Even if only one deep slice group can attend a workshop, they have a responsibility to take home the self managing workplace concepts and process, and the tentative design, in order to participatively produce a final design from the whole unit.

Parallel Workshops – The Series. You can organise a series of parallel workshops for large organisation redesigns. Each workshop may include people from different parts of the organisation, all working to redesign the whole organisation. This allows you to include everyone in the redesign process and still keep your doors open for business. The series of parallel workshops can occur simultaneously or over an extended time. Consolidation of several designs into one final design can be done when the workshops have been completed.

Each participative design workshop occurs over one and a half or two days, depending on the design. A typical workshop has anywhere from 24-30 participants from the organisation. At the beginning of the workshop, participants sort themselves into four small design groups. Each group is composed of a cross section of the whole organisation being designed – a deep slice. A typical small group may have 6-8 people workers from various sections and a supervisor or manager. The task is to design the workplace to be self managing. A workplace could be a manufacturing plant, a store, a service centre, a school, or any significant part of a larger organisation.

For example, one hi-tech manufacturing plant used a series of participative design workshops to involve all 150 workers and managers in the redesign effort. There were three workshops, each one including a cross section – deep slice – of the whole plant. The designs that resulted from the workshops were communicated to everyone at 'town meetings.' Then volunteers, using feedback gathered at the 'town meetings,' integrated the various designs into a final design, that the workforce approved.

Up the Hierarchy. In organizations with many levels of hierarchy it is useful to do workshops that start at the bottom and go up the hierarchy. Workshops begin at the operational level, then proceed to supervisory and mid-management levels, and conclude with a workshop for top management. Each participative design workshop contains at least two levels of the existing hierarchy.

This variation applies when an organisation has decided to systematically change to self management. Such a decision means that senior management will change to self management too. Middle managers can participate in the workshops at the worker level and also the senior management level, providing an overlapping perspective.

Overlapping workshops assure workers that top management is serious about the systemic nature of the change. It also allows each level of the organisation to design a self managing structure and determine what work it is responsible for controlling and coordinating. Workers often suspect that redesign happens only at the bottom of the organisation and that management will not change itself.

Educational Workshops. It is often useful to do workshops strictly for the purpose of introducing people to the concepts and methods of the self managing workplace. Managers and workers sometimes prefer to test drive the workshop to determine whether doing it for real is right for them. For purposes of education, the workshop should include the briefings on design principles and a hands-on experience of the workshop tools.

Chapter 6

Rebuilding The Land Bank of South Africa

This real life story describes in detail how one organisation used participative design workshops to redesign into a self managing workplace. All the features of the workshop are present here. The Land Bank used the term 'organisation rebuilding' to describe their application of the participative design workshop.

The Setting

It's Monday morning in Lichtenburg, a city in the North West province of South Africa. This is farm country. The maize is knee high on this hot summer day in January; it's a bumper crop for the Afrikaner farmers of the region. It's also a year in which emergent black farmers are breaking into the agriculture business, restoring a way of life that predates white settlement. Change is in the air everywhere in South Africa now. What happens this week in Lichtenburg could change the way farming is financed in the area for a long time.

Two newly trained workshop leaders enter the Lichtenburg Land and Agriculture Bank branch building in the centre of town. They are Bankies Malan and Shameela Kahn. Bankies is an agricultural economist, who normally works in the Port Elizabeth branch. Shameela is an accounts clerk in the Rustenburg bank, next town over from Lichtenburg. I am here to support Bankies and Shameela as they do their first workshop. The Land and Agriculture Bank is called the Land Bank for short, and its role is to provide affordable financing to farmers and farm co-operatives – loans for buying property, equipment, and crops.

The week before, Bankies and Shameela, along with eighteen other Land Bank staff from around the country, were trained to do the participative design workshop. Now they are ready to do it. The Land Bank decided to have its own workers lead the redesign effort. They call it capacity building. Better to build deep levels of skill and knowledge in self management, than to rely on external consultants. Capacity building means the Bank will have the internal skills to sustain the change over the years to come. The union has been involved in the overall planning of the change, and a union leader is a key member of the workshop leader team. Today, five branch banks – Bloemfontein, Port Elizabeth, Pretoria, Ermelo, and here in Lichtenburg – are starting participative design workshops, all led by workers from the Land Bank. The schedule calls for five banks to do work-place redesign each week for the next five weeks.

The branch director meets us in the lobby. His name is Wim Alberts and this is his first day as branch director. He shows us into his office and we smell fresh white paint on the walls. Wim says, 'Enough of the musty, dull colours of the past. Things are going to change around here. I am very excited to be here and am anxious to meet the people.' Wim was just promoted from his mid-management position in another branch to this new job. He has been preparing himself for this kind of leadership challenge for years. He is a colonel in the South African military reserves and believes team management is the only way to go. The old job description of branch manager was an administrative position. The new branch director will need to be a business strategist, skilled in leadership, business planning, and marketing – an ambassador for the bank. Starting March 1, just six weeks away, every branch bank becomes an autonomous business unit responsible for its own budget and performance. The workshops this week will pave the way.

We go over the schedule of activities for the upcoming week with Wim. In a few minutes Wim will meet the workers for the first time. Then Bankies and Shameela will spend a couple of hours briefing people on the workplace rebuilding workshops, telling them about the purpose of the workshops, the schedule of activities, and the design principles. Workshops begin Tuesday morning and end Friday afternoon; everyone will participate. The workshops are so important that the bank will shut down its usual business for the week. Walk in business is infrequent; most of the bank's client business is done in the field.

The Lichtenburg branch office is a scene from the past – a monolithic building of the 1950s with institutional dull green walls, and outdated machines and equipment. Filing cabinets are everywhere. It's a paper driven operation, with little evidence of computers – just a few here and there. Competition lurks around ever corner as private sector banks are quickly moving into the agriculture marketplace. The need for the bank to modernise, both in terms of technology and people development, is paramount.

Wim leaves us to go meet the workers. Bankies and Shameela fill me in on the old Land Bank culture. It's an autocratic story. The branch manager sat in his office checking other people's work. Most decisions, particularly those involving major loan applications, were taken in Pretoria, the head office. The branch manager had little elbow room, and very limited responsibilities. People below had even less autonomy. Until this organisational transformation effort, the Land Bank's mission was to provide affordable loans to white Afrikaner farmers. The Land Bank is a parastatal institution, but is not dependent on tax payer money. The bank earns its money from interest income. It was one of the mainstay institutions of the Apartheid years. Now new leadership came and with it a new mission – to broaden the bank's customer base to include emergent black farmers, keeping its 'bread and butter' white clientele, and doing it all profitably and efficiently.

Bankies and Shameela conduct two briefings to prepare people for the workshops so they know what to expect. Half the staff of 36 people attends each meeting. After some initial reticence, people ask questions. Most of the questions have to do with pay and security. 'Will anyone lose their job? What happens to section heads? What about promotions and pay?' Most of the concerns come from veteran male workers, especially the section heads, who are just now realising what a flattened hierarchy means to them. The younger people, especially the women, are upbeat and excited about new possibilities. The Land Bank is a union operation. Union leaders have been involved in the overall project for some time and support the changes.

Day One: An Era Ends

The workplace rebuilding workshop begins Tuesday morning at 8:30. We clear a space in the middle of the work area on the first floor. Desks and file cabinets are shoved aside and chairs arranged in a circle. The branch director Wim will answer the phone and deal with pressing business issues during the week. Wim introduces the workshop, expressing his commitment to the change to self management. He tells everyone that it's up to them to redesign their work.

Wim has negotiated the following arrangement with the staff. Everyone will come into work at the usual 7:30 a.m. start time. They will do their bank work for one hour, then move into workshop mode. There is a one hour lunch period at 1:00 p.m., followed by another hour of normal bank work. The last hour will be more workshop, ending the day at 4:00 p.m. People are happy with this arrangement because it allows them to get some work done, and it does not interfere with family obligations after work hours.

Bankies and Shameela review the agenda with participants. They also introduce and discuss the minimum critical specifications that will guide the redesign process. These specifications come from the series of search conferences done around the country to re-envision the vision, purpose, and mission of the Land Bank. Specifications also came from the bank's Board of Directors. At the Land Bank these specifications are called the Framework.

FRAMEWORK

* Increase clients by 15% over 3 years
* Cost effective
* No increase in operational costs
* Multi-skilled self managing teams
* Cover skills shortage with training,
     adding skills wherever possible
* Flatter structure with streamlined administration
* Customer focus with direct customer delivery
* Branch & team empowerment
* People development & increased job satisfaction

AGENDA

REDESIGNING THE BRANCH BANK

Tuesday
- Introduction & Expectations
- Briefing: Design Principles
  - The Bureaucratic & Self Managing Workplaces
- Six Criteria for Productive Work — Assessment
- Skills Required — Assessment
- Redesign of the Branch
  - Current Work Flow & Organisation Chart
  - Redesign the Branch

Wednesday
- Redesign of the Branch — Continued
- Agreement on Branch Design
- Choosing of New Terms

BUILDING NEW TEAMS

Thursday
- Six Criteria for Productive Work
- Skills Required on the New Team
- Work Flow of the Team
- Team Goals & Measures
- Training Plan

Friday
- Team Control & Coordination
- Team External Relations
- Resource Needs
- Review Six Criteria

A letter went out to all workers from the managing director Dr. Helena Dolny clarifying some of the design specifications. Dr. Dolny also made video tape presentations to deal with workers' concerns about the changes. The letter and videos make these three points. People had this information going into the workshops.

1. The framework and design specifications are non-negotiable. No more layers of management; no more working in separate sections. There should be only two levels of structure in each branch – a branch director and self managing teams. We want a different way of working that is more democratic, giving more responsibility to people doing the work. We want an open culture in the bank where people can be brave, disagree, and contribute to the success of the business.

2. The Land Bank is overstaffed. We have a large staff relative to our current business. For now that means we have excess capacity that is available for training and for growing the business. We need different kinds of jobs, not different people. As the bank identifies new types of business and modernises, new work opportunities will open up for people. Some jobs will become obsolete, others created. Retrenchment is the last option.

3. The salary system will change, but there will be no salary loss due to redesign. Pay and promotion will be based on skill and performance, not length of service. A bonus system will be developed to reward productivity. Regarding affirmative action, women and blacks have been held back in favour of white males for too long. The bank has had affirmative action for white males for years. Workers are encouraged to participate, join in the redesign, and find the right niche for themselves.

Helena Dolny has been managing director of the Land Bank for about one year. She has a Ph.D. in agricultural economics. She and her husband Joe Slovo lived in political exile in Mozambique for many years because of their anti-Apartheid activism. During their years away from South Africa, both Joe and Helena continued their political activity. Joe Slovo, before his death in 1995, was leader of the South African communist party and was legal advisor to Nelson Mandela and the African National Congress (ANC) for more than thirty years.

The appointment of Helena Dolny as managing director of this Apartheid institution, and her leadership in expanding the Land Bank's mission to benefit black farmers, has workers wondering about the future of their jobs. After all, most workers are male Afrikaners. Throughout, Dr. Dolny communicates her commitment to making the Land Bank competitive and profitable through its people. Workers in the Land Bank are having to adjust to Dr. Dolny's leadership philosophy which is egalitarian and direct. In the past, the bank's managing directors were Afrikaner men who maintained an elite, patriarchal status. People tell stories of how the elevator in the Pretoria head office would have to empty to make room for the managing director. Helena Dolny, on the other hand, talks directly with workers at every level, expecting to exchange views bluntly and honestly without repercussions. People are not used to being treated as adults.

After Bankies and Shameela fully discuss the agenda, people work in small groups to list their expectations for the week. We hear more questions about pay in the new team environment and job security. There is also excitement and disbelief that this is for real. We find it necessary to address the pay and security issues frequently during the workshops, reminding people that the Land Bank is committed to developing its workers and expanding its business. Down deep everyone wonders whether there are too many people for the workload of the branch bank. It's hard for people to believe their jobs are not in jeopardy.

Bankies does a briefing on the two design principles – the bureaucratic and self managing workplaces – then introduces the six criteria for productive work. Small groups form. Each small group is a cross section of the whole bank conveyancing (title transfer), loans, typing, recoveries, accounts, and sundries. People who were section heads and assistant managers are also spread around various groups. The groups are loose and playful during this activity. The scores indicate an organisation where decision making and goal setting are far away from the workers. Jobs are segmented and boring, particularly for typists and people handling paper work. Section heads and agricultural economists are the only ones who see the whole loan process beginning to end. Most people are confused about the future at the Land Bank because of the changes going on in Pretoria and change in South Africa broadly speaking. Bankies and Shameela help the group understand the usefulness of the exercise. If the Land Bank is going to survive and even thrive, the bank must be designed so that each worker's productivity needs are satisfied.

At about midmorning, we begin the skills assessment. The small groups brainstorm all the skills required to get the work of the branch done. The products of the four groups are compared and several people volunteer to quickly merge to one final skills list. Then the small groups complete their own skills matrix, making appropriate marks for no skill, some skill, and high skills. These matrices are presented and the whole group compares the lists and draws conclusions about where the organisation's strengths and weaknesses are regarding current skill development.

The skills assessment indicates a workplace where many people are deskilled. Typists (all women) can type but, despite their knowledge, are not allowed to process loans. Loan processors know how to do the loan application process, but cannot type or use a computer. Agricultural economists are highly educated and are skilled at analysing the risks of loan applicants in the field. People skilled in conveyancing know how to do the legal tasks of title research but lack the educational background of the agricultural economists. Perhaps with a little training, they could handle some of the skills of the agricultural economist. Maybe loan processors could learn some aspects of field evaluation work as well. Recovery workers have the skill to assess why a loan fails and know how to structure loans for repayment; maybe their skill could be useful during the loan approval process.

Redesign work begins at noon. People go back into their small design groups and start by drawing a diagram of the current organisation chart, then they draw the work flow of how loans move through the bank. The current organisational structure of the Lichtenburg branch is the usual hierarchical arrangement. Below the branch manager, people are split into functions called sections. There's a section for conveyancing, agricultural economics, accounts, loans, recoveries, and sundry (black servants who clean the building and serve tea). Each section is supervised by a section head, all of whom are men who worked their way up into the position. Their job is to control the work of those below. The section heads have little decision making authority, and must go to the branch manager for most approvals. Below the section heads are supervisors who check other people's work looking for mistakes.

The groups have trouble drawing the branch's organisation chart, as no one ever saw the official version. No one, except the section heads, ever gave much thought to organisation design to begin with. Drawing the bank's work flow is even more of a challenge, but because each group is made up of people from every section, they are able to put the puzzle pieces together. People enjoy seeing the whole picture for the first time, and this is a lively exercise. What they see is a loan conveyor belt, just like a factory assembly line, full of wasted steps and much opportunity for improvement.

Each group starts discussing options for redesigning the branch into self managing teams. There is considerable energy for this task, and no shortage of confusion about what's possible. Bankies and Shameela help the groups by exploring some basic design options with them. For example, they consider the pros and cons of designing multi-skilled teams made up of people who now have conveyancing, typing, loan, and account skills. This option means that eventually everyone could learn all the skills involved in making a loan. Another option would separate conveying out as a separate team because the skills are complex, and the conveyancing workers have optimal scores on variety in the six criteria assessment.

The day ends with each team presenting its incomplete design ideas. There is a spirited large group discussion, lots of energy and heat. We ask the teams to give interim reports of their unfinished work so as to encourage them to really listen to one another. If they had finished their designs, chances are each group would have been more defensive of their own designs. This way, people get to hear different design ideas, then go home and sleep on it.

During the workshop, Wim busies himself handling bank business. He comes into the workshop room periodically, encouraging people and listening to the group's progress. The decision was taken at the beginning of the week that Wim would not directly participate in the workshop, leaving the design of the work to the workers themselves. At one point during a break in the action, the loan section head went into Wim's office to get him to approve a loan application. He needed Wim's signature. Wim quickly gave the form back to the branch head without signing it. 'You sign it!' says Wim. The loan person looked back in horror, saying, 'I cannot do it; it is not my job. I am not authorised.' Wim took a blank piece of paper and wrote: 'I, Wim Alberts, do hereby authorise this branch team member to approve this loan with his own signature.' Wim gave him the paper, and the one time section head signed it. Things change.

Day Two: A New Workplace Design Emerges

Everyone is ready to get to work Wednesday morning. We begin with a large group discussion about the design possibilities presented Tuesday afternoon. There were more similarities among the four designs than differences. All designs called for multi-skilled teams. The main difference was the size and number of teams, and the nature of work that these teams would be responsible for doing. The key debate centred on the make up of the loan teams. Should the agricultural economists be on loan teams or be a separate specialist team? What about conveyancing? Is the conveyancing function too complex and difficult for a multi-skilled loan team to take on, or should conveyancing be its own team as well?

The agricultural economist function is currently a process bottleneck. When it's time in the overall loan application process for a risk analysis, loan application staff must stop and wait for the economist to do his work. Lichtenburg, like other branches, is understaffed in agricultural economics and there is a lack of training for others who could do some part of the economist's job. On the other hand, some argue it's best for specialists to do evaluations. Assessments should be done by outsiders to the teams to keep the process objective. Every design group comes up with the second option – keep the agricultural economists as specialists, but expect them to train people on the loan teams to do some of the assessment work.

The argument about what to do with conveyancing is hot. The conveyancing staff are responsible for drawing up deeds for the transfer of land ownership. The job has significant legal consequences and there is little room for error. Like agricultural economics, conveyancing is also a process bottleneck making the loan process less efficient. In the end, all teams decide to put conveyancing in the multi-skilled loan teams. The main reason is to provide more variety for workers and to give the loan teams ownership of the entire loan process, including conveyancing.

The other question involved the work of the black sundry staff. Despite encouragement from the group and low scores on the six criteria assessment, the black workers do not want to be on multi-skilled teams. Bankies and Shameela talk with them to make sure their views were expressed. This part of the design concerned us. There must be a way for the black sundry workers to have a good job.

By mid morning, the large group agreed on one design that incorporates the work of the four small design groups. Members of each small group volunteer to go off in another room and draw a final design diagram. The rest of the 36 people work simultaneously in a large group to decide how to choose teams. As it turns out, many of the old section heads and male work leaders go off to draw the final diagram, leaving some of the younger men and women to work out the team selection. For the first time in the workshop women jump up to the flip chart to lead the discussion. Things are changing now.

After about one hour both groups are finished working. The design group comes back with this diagram that they explain to the rest of the workers (see next page).

The final design features two loan teams that are multi-skilled. The teams would be composed of people who now are limited to typing, conveyancing, loan processing, and recoveries. The two agricultural economists become their own team, and part of their new responsibility is to educate the loan teams to do some risk assessment work themselves. Filing and accounting are the work of the records team, an important administrative function supporting the loan teams. All teams are led by the branch director. This is a big change as the director will now work with teams, not individual workers. A special training and development team will be in place temporarily to get people up to speed with new skills. And the tea service and cleaning continue to be the work of the black sundry workers, now a self managing team. The entrepreneurial spirit and participation of the black sundry workers suggest an even more interesting idea. Perhaps the sundry workers could become their own business, cleaning and servicing the branch banks, and other organisations in Lichtenburg too. This idea will be explored in the weeks ahead.

NEW LAND BANK DESIGN — LICHTENBURG

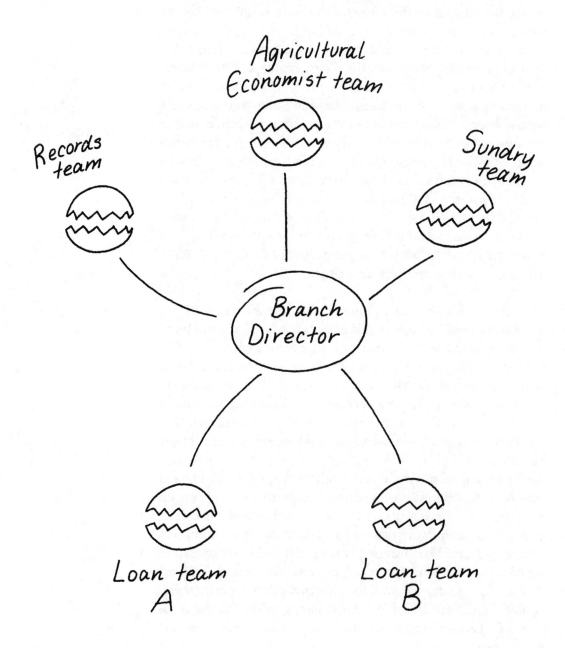

Agricultural
Economist team

Records
team

Sundry
team

Branch
Director

Loan team
A

Loan team
B

The whole group goes into what we can only call a dialogue session to process the design. We call it dialogue because the conversation is characterised by intense listening, low voices, and a flow of conversation from one person to another. We hear lots of voices in the room that were not heard before, particularly women, the younger men, and the blacks. Everyone is deeply processing the design together, exploring how it would actually work.

Towards the end of these 45 minutes of conversation, a debate breaks out. A couple of the conveyancing staff balk at the idea of being part of a multi-skilled group. This happens even though each design group, with conveyancing people participating, decided to put conveyancing into the loan teams. Some of the conveyancing people are having second thoughts. After a long, difficult argument back and forth that did not result in any kind of consensus, the group decides to put it to a vote. The result: 31 for putting conveyancing in the loan team, 5 for making conveyancing its own team. After the vote, people ask the five dissenters to give the design a try. They agree, but promise to continue to be critics. The design is finished and everyone is excited to see what happens next. Spirits are high.

The group that was working on team selection gives its report. It used the skills assessment to split people into the multi-skilled loan teams. There is considerable discussion in a large group about the assignments and some switches are made to make sure the teams are balanced by skill. It's interesting to see how seriously and responsibly people are treating this important step.

The other teams are easier to staff. What's more difficult to resolve is the question of how loan applications flow into the new team system. How do we fairly decide which loan team gets which clients? Should we use the alphabet to do it? For example – clients A-M go to one team, clients N-Z to the other team? Or should we do it by type of loan? Perhaps different teams organise around different loan products, or geographic regions. What to do? This debate would go on for the rest of the workshop and be unresolved until the end.

Chapter 6
Rebuilding
The Land Bank
of South Africa

Just before breaking for lunch, the group calls their branch director, Wim Alberts, into the room to listen to their ideas for design. Wim listens carefully to the design. He asks some clarifying questions, suggests some minor improvements, and says wholeheartedly, 'Let's do it!' At the end of the day, there is still more discussion and some last minute changes in team assignments. Then we end the first workshop and tell people to come back ready in the morning to start working in their new teams. The branch design took a total of eight working hours to complete, not including lunch, tea time, and bank work.

The Launch

Thursday morning starts with Bankies and Shameela reviewing the agenda for the next two days – the building new teams workshop. In this workshop, people get into their new teams and go through some of the same assessments from the first workshop. New activities are added to help them get thoroughly organised as a team. New self managing teams need to set realistic, challenging goals for productivity and team development. The new teams also need to set procedures for effectively controlling and coordinating their own work, something the section heads used to do. And they need to sort out positive working relationships with other groups, clients, and management.

The new teams start with a review of their six criteria for productive work assessment from the branch rebuild workshop. The assignment for the group, this time, is to have each person talk about how their needs were or were not satisfied in the old design, and what their hopes are for the new team. All but one of the teams jumps to this task and has spirited discussions and lots of fun. One of the new loan teams goes headlong into conflict, with people disagreeing. Separate conversations happen, and a couple of people tune out altogether. From the outside it looks like a power struggle. Shameela intervenes. After exploring what was happening, it becomes clear that the team is still not comfortable that it had the right skills to do the work.

With a little encouragement from Shameela, the team publicly expresses its concern in plenary that the two loan teams are
not balanced by skill properly. There is more discussion of the
issue, and people feel comfortable the issue has been fully
addressed and now we can get on with our work. We are wondering how many times this issue will recycle until the teams
are happy with their composition.

Wim Alberts comes into the workshop room and asks for a
few minutes of time before tea break. He announces to the group,
'On next Monday, I want you all to come to work in tackies, jeans,
and T-shirts. We are going to rearrange the office so that teams have
their own work space.' Everyone in the room spontaneously breaks
into applause. People appreciate Wim's commitment.

The teams then proceed to draw up their own skill matrix
and work flow charts. The work flow activity helps everyone,
particularly in the loan teams, understand the scope of work the
new team is responsible for doing. Doing the skills matrix calms
the fears of the loan teams. There are more double tick marks
than they expected. They are in good shape to start taking
responsibility for the loan process. They also can see they have
considerable resources on the team to do their own training.

It's mid morning and time for the teams to work on more
organising tasks. The task is for each group to set goals at three
levels: team performance goals, team development goals, and
goals for individual development. These goals must be measurable and time bounded. For starters, teams are encouraged to
develop one or two team performance goals. Expecting new
teams coming out of a bureaucratic work environment to set
goals is challenging to everyone. It's also critical to the success
of the teams. Ordinarily, management has a clear set of goals in
place. The teams set their own goals within the framework of
the broader performance goals of the organisation. In the Land
Bank, branch directors were just now getting the responsibility
for setting performance goals for their branch. In the past, all
goal setting was done at the head office in Pretoria and the
branches were expected to comply. Branch managers were
merely workplace supervisors charged with controlling the
work of the branch.

Wim gives the group the context upon which the Land Bank is operating regarding goals. He says he and the Pretoria head office will be finalising branch goals within a matter of weeks. For now, he encouraged the groups to experiment with team performance goal setting, and we will continue to refine and improve them together over time. With this encouragement, the groups go to work on goals. Wim is now spending more time in the workshop, moving from team to team, encouraging and listening to people as they form the new work structure.

Thursday ends with teams beginning to put together comprehensive training plans. These plans are based on the skills assessment done earlier, as well as the team and individual goal setting activity. Teams are asked to emphasise those skills they can train each other on the job, not waiting for training to come from head office. Everyone leaves in good mood, ready for the braai (cookout) hosted by the Land Bank that evening.

Many staff members bring their families to the braai Thursday evening. People relax around the fire, enjoying good food, drink, and conversation. Several people have the same question. 'Where did these ideas come from? We never heard of anything like it in our lives.' We say, 'What do you mean, these ideas?' One of the section heads, now team member, says, 'We never heard of teams taking responsibility and being accountable for work. At first it seemed crazy that I would be in a team. Now I kind of like it. Where did it come from?' We gladly tell them the story of the British coal mines and the history of self managing work groups. What seemed unreal to people on Monday, looks promising on this warm, starry evening on the Land Bank lawn.

Day Four: A New Era Begins

The work on Friday is almost entirely self managing. Bankies and Shameela introduce a series of organising tasks and the groups work at their own pace. The tasks have the teams developing internal agreements for how to coordinate their work together, how to work with other parts of the Land Bank and clients, and to make sure they have the resources to do their work as a team.

The teams' plans for how to control and coordinate their work are comprehensive. They include agreements on how to handle everything from work assignments to sick time and holidays, to documentation of team responsibilities and schedules. The loan teams finalise their arrangement for deciding which team works with which clients. One team takes responsibility for the first half of the alphabet, the other team the remainder all the way to Z. In plenary, all teams agree to weekly all staff meetings every Monday morning to get off to a good start.

The teams finish all their organising tasks by lunch time and report their results in plenary. Although the workshop is coming to an end, it doesn't feel as if anything is finished. Just the opposite. There is a strong sense among the workers that we are only just beginning a new adventure at work. Wim Alberts closes the workshop by thanking everyone for their energetic participation. He reminds people about Monday. It will be a day for teams to rearrange the office. The two new loan teams are going to be located in their own work spaces beginning Monday. New pay systems are down the road. There will be skill based pay for the self managing teams and a bonus system to reward the branch for productivity and generating new business. Bankies and Shameela leave, knowing the Lichtenburg branch bank is in better shape then it was Monday morning. Next week, and the weeks to follow, they and their fellow facilitators will repeat the workplace rebuilding workshop process in all 25 branches of the Land Bank.

Epilogue

In five days, the Lichtenburg branch bank transformed itself from a bureaucratic workplace to a team based organisation designed to better serve clients – Afrikaners and emergent black farmers. The new self managing workplace is also designed to meet workers' needs for being productive members of their organisation. People are now responsible for their own decisions and goals. They have a structure that is variety increasing, where everyone sees the loan process beginning to end. With training plans in hand and the promise of a new pay and reward system, people are beginning to see a worthwhile future at the Land Bank. By March 1, all 25 branch banks are rebuilt following the same participative design workshop approach as Lichtenburg. No two branch banks look exactly alike in design. Each has a workforce with unique human needs, and its own unique business environment.

Land Bank Goals and New Compensation System
by Nancy Cebula

While the 25 branch banks were doing their redesign workshops, the leaders of the Land Bank were busy completing organisation-wide strategic goals. These goals permeate the organisation, with each level – province, branch bank, teams – setting and negotiating their own nested goals to bring the strategy into reality. Here's one example.

One of the objectives of the 'new' Land Bank is to assist the Ministry of Agriculture in its goal of increasing the number of farms owned and operated by historically disadvantaged farmers. 'Historically disadvantaged' is defined as those who were denied the right to own property under the previous Apartheid System. For example, blacks, coloureds, and Indians were not allowed to own land under Apartheid.

The Land Bank has translated this into a goal: 'Provide financial support for historically disadvantaged farmers.' To work toward achieving this goal, the Land Bank developed a program called 'Step Up Loans.' The Step Up program is aimed at providing loans to black farmers who want to buy land, equipment, seeds, and transportation to market. It includes an education component for branches in many small villages to provide accounts for the loan recipients. The purpose is to make distribution of the loan money easier and to facilitate repayment of the loan.

The branch directors set goals in each of the nine provinces of South Africa to provide for the increased support for black farmers. The branch directors in each province then negotiated with each other the number of Step Up loans that each branch should have as a goal. This was based on the amount of land (particularly smallholdings) for sale, the number of potential black farmers in the region, agricultural conditions, such as droughts, and other considerations.

At the branch level, the newly formed loan teams developed their own team goals to help the branch and Land Bank succeed in this goal area. Some examples of loan team goals are these:

'Step Up information will be made available to black farmers in the local languages – Sotho, Zulu, and Tswana, by January 1.'

'Our team will do at least 10 education field visits each month to black owned farms and co-operatives to make them aware of Land Bank services.'

'Three team members will learn to speak Sotho by January 1.'

'Each team member will learn to speak at least one African language by June.'

The Land Bank's New Compensation System
by Nancy Cebula

The compensation system in the 'old' Land Bank was one of entitlement. There were 17 levels of pay with 3 steps in each level. Only white men could move beyond the third level. People received automatic increases every year, regardless of competency or performance. A Christmas bonus was paid annually.

The Land Bank's new mission and team based structure required the complete redesign of the compensation system. At the time this book went to press, the Land Bank's new compensation system was not yet finished. So, the following descriptions are speculative, based on the development of the system to this point.

The new compensation system being developed is based on skills and knowledge held, performance and competency, and includes a bonus plan to reward team and organisation-wide performance. Race and gender no longer determine pay.

A skill based pay system makes sense in a self managing workplace because it encourages people to become multi-skilled to the extent that the team needs it. In the self managing workplace, the more you know and the more you can do, the more valuable you are to yourself, your team, and the overall organisation.

Broad Banding

Broad banding is a way of bundling together skills and knowledge, and assigning monetary value to them. There are to be 5 bands of skills and knowledge in the Land Bank's new compensation system. These are: senior executive skills (sr exec); technical speciality skills (tech spec); business development advisory skills (BDA); administrative/accounting skills (admin/acc't); and support skills. Below is an illustration of the Land Bank's 5 broad bands:

	Sr Exec	Tech Spec	BDA	Admin/ Acc't	Support

People

In

Charge

Within each of the 5 bands are different levels of skills and knowledge. For example, the skills that are to be measured in the support band are shown in the diagram below.

					Level 5:
					Level 4:
					Level 3:
					Level 2:
					Level 1:
Teams Working Skills	Word Processing Skills	Customer Service Skills	Language Fluency Skills	Product Knowledge	

The bottom row of the band identifies the skills to be measured. The columns show the proficiency levels for each skill.

A monetary amount (in Rand) is assigned to each of the levels in each band. These numbers are based on information from market surveys. A competency test is being developed for each level of each skill in the bands. In addition to the competency tests, 360 degree evaluations are to be used to determine whether or not a person can use the skill in a practical manner. They are called '360 degree' because the evaluations include feedback from up, down, outside (all around) the worker.

Now let's see how the compensation system applies to the branch bank team based designs. A typical branch team design looks like this:

Branch Director

Loan Processing Team #1	Loan Processing Team #2	Loan Processing Team #3	Accounting/ Auditing Team	Help Desk Team

Loan processing team members are to be compensated in the business development advisory skills (BDA) band. Accounting /auditing team members are compensated in the administrative /accounting skills band. Help desk team members are rewarded in the support skills band. The branch director is covered under the senior executive skill band.

In addition to the 25 branch banks around the country, the Land Bank has a head office that provides support and administrative services to the branches. Staff in the head office are experts in various technical areas, such as law and finance. They are to be compensated in the technical speciality skills band. There are some workers in the head office whose skills and knowledge are in the administrative /accounting skills and support skills bands. Senior executive skills are required for senior management positions in the head office and for branch director positions.

Skilled team members are working with human resources and senior executives to develop the skill bands, the competency tests, and performance (behavioural) standards.

Team and Organisation-wide Bonuses

Self managing workplaces typically share their financial success with everyone in the organisation through team and organisation-wide bonuses. In the bonus system being developed at the Land Bank, bonuses are to be paid to everyone in the organisation, based on the organisation's success at achieving identified goals.

The bonus system works like this. The goals to be measured to determine success are set at the beginning of the plan. These goals reflect the strategic intent of the Land Bank and are time bounded. Monetary values, often percentages of salary, are assigned to the goals and measures. The bonus plan is communicated to all workers so they understand what the potential bonuses are.

Bonuses are paid only when the whole organisation meets its goals. Once it is determined that the bank's goals are met, then bonuses flow down through the organisation. Each branch bank and the departments at the head office pay out bonuses if they have reached their goals. Likewise, each team is paid a bonus if it has met its team goals.

Goals and measures are reviewed regularly to ensure they still are an accurate measure of the strategic intent. The bonuses are to be paid frequently enough that workers can see the connection between their own daily performance and the success of the Land Bank.

The skill based pay and team bonus systems work hand in hand to reinforce the design of the Land Bank. The change to self management provides people a workplace design that satisfies their need to be productive. The compensation system rewards them financially for co-operative, customer focused behaviour on the job.

Self managing workplace design has been one phase in a larger organisation transformation effort at the Land Bank, all led by managing director Dr. Helena Dolny. Credit goes to South African consultant Steve Hobbs for bringing self managing workplace design to the Land Bank. Also providing consulting were Clint Whyte, Nancy Cebula, and Tom Devane.

Shameela Kahn and Bankies Malan were part of a team of eighteen workplace rebuilding workshop leaders. This is a brave and skilful group of Land Bank employees. They are: Sello Segalwe, Joe Barclay, Tinus Prinsloo, Morne du Plessis, Andrea Dedekind, Ken Delport, Andre Scholtemeyer, Hannes Venter, David Hoyle, Deowald van Loggerenberg, Alta van Wyk, Salome De Beer, Joel Mekwa, Rodney Augustine, Jennifer du Preez, and Piet Moolman.

Thanks to Wim Alberts and all the staff at the Lichtenburg branch bank for being the stars in this story.

Bankies Malan *presented the Land Bank Story at the European Ecology of Work Conference in Bonn, Germany in 1999.*

E-mail: whmalan@landbank.co.za

Chapter 7

Getting The Conditions Right For Workplace Design

The participative design workshops at the Land Bank did not just happen overnight. Months of hard work provided a foundation that made it possible for the change to happen. Designing a self managing workplace starts a long time before anyone sets foot inside a participative design workshop. Like anything else in life, good preparation is essential before you embark upon a big project, whether it's a long journey or a structural change in your organisation.

Getting the conditions right for organisation change may take as much time as the change itself. We know organisations that have taken anywhere from three months to one year of preparation before starting participative design workshops. The conditions for successful workplace design and implementation are: management commitment; clarity about the work to be redesigned; minimum critical specifications to guide the design process; proper preparation of the workforce; and design of the workshops.

Management commitment. While the redesign workshops happen at the bottom of the organisation and work their way up, the overall process begins at the top. The best approach is for the managing director or top executive and their team to make the decision to change to self management and communicate their commitment throughout the entire organisation, no matter how large. Then the divisions and various departments of the enterprise begin adapting workplace design to their local needs. Doing design this way provides system wide change. Experience teaches us that structural change done in only a part of a bigger system, like a corporation, risks failure because of the resistance that comes from the rest of the organisation.

Nevertheless, we know many success stories of self managing workplace design done in part of a corporation or large organisation. Examples in this book show how successful design happened in: a local wine production facility that is part of a larger corporation; one factory in a hi-tech company; a call centre in an assurance company; and do-it-yourself stores in a large parent organisation. While the system wide change strategy is conceptually right, our experience is that, from a practical point of view, many successful change projects occur at the unit level of bigger organisational systems. Self managing workplace design is no exception.

The keys to successful workplace design at the unit level are clear. The unit should be a stand alone part of the larger organisation, such as a factory, service centre, school, or division like research and development. It is best if the unit considering changing to self management is not made up of work processes that overlap with other divisions of the same organisation. The unit undergoing the change should, to the extent possible, control its own work processes. The unit should have lots of decision making power and the authorisation from higher up the chain that changing to self management is OK. We have seen too many workplace designs snuffed out early on by surprised executives who were not part of the decision to change to a self managing workplace.

Regardless of whether the unit of redesign is the corporation or a school, the decision to change to self management starts at the top. Making this important decision means that the managers are fully educated about the design principles and committed to making the change. At this early stage it is also critical to involve the unions. Changing to a self managing workplace requires the full support and commitment of union leadership and full participation of the rank and file members.

Management should be clear about why it wants to change to a self managing workplace. The best reason for doing workplace design is to improve the performance of the organisation through its people. Workplace design is not a way to downsize the workforce. Workers should not be expected to design themselves out of a job. Experience teaches that during the first couple of years of implementation, self managing workplaces need extra resources to allow for the training often required for multi-skilling. Self managing workplace design is not a method for producing a happy, content workforce. While you can expect workers to report improved satisfaction after implementing their own designs, the purpose of change is to improve quality and productivity. Happiness is not an end in itself.

Management should also be aware that human resource practices and systems need to change to make the new self managing workplace successful. Self managing groups take responsibility for everything from selecting new members to being fully involved in disciplinary processes. Typically, self managing groups are most effective when they have skill based pay systems and the opportunity to share in the monetary success of the organisation.

When introducing top managers to self management, it is useful to have them experience the participative design workshop as an educational way to learn about the concepts and method. Managers sometimes prefer to test drive the workshop to determine whether doing it for real is right for them. An educational participative design workshop includes the briefings on design principles and a hands on experience of the workshop activities.

Clarity about strategy and work. The next question management explores before embarking on workplace design is whether the organisation has a clear strategic plan laying out the direction and work of the organisation over the years to come. If the organisation has no up to date strategy, or if the plan was done without a thorough examination of the changing conditions in the organisation's environment, then do some planning. We suggest using a search conference, the participative planning

83

Chapter 7
Getting the
Conditions
right for
Workplace
Design

method developed by the same people who gave us the participative design workshop.

Having a clear strategy, direction, and desirable future for the organisation has implications for workplace design. At the Land Bank of South Africa, search conferences led to a redefinition of some of the basic work of the branch banks, changing the nature of some loans and expanding the bank's customer base. This new strategy was fed into the participative design workshops to help workers better understand the changing nature of the work.[1]

On the down side, we know of a manufacturing plant in a large corporation that bypassed the planning step and went straight ahead to workplace design. One month into implementation of the new design, corporate headquarters pulled the plug and sent the manufacturing operation to an Asian country. Failure to scan changes in their business environment led to frustration for management and workers alike.

Minimum critical specification. Management (along with the union) develops guidelines for the design process. These guidelines describe what design features are open or not open to change, such as organisation policy and strategy limitations, or budget constraints. We call these guidelines minimum critical specifications.

Before launching a workplace redesign effort, it is important for management to clearly identify the limitations and boundaries of the process. These limitations and boundaries act as the minimum critical specifications that guide the redesign. An example of a design specification that is minimum and critical is self management. Organisations that want to change to self management should clearly state this expectation as a specification up front. It is also a good idea for management to specify that the new design satisfy people's human needs as expressed in the six criteria for productive work exercise. The design should give people a job that is worthwhile.

When designing a workplace, specify what is essential for the system to be self managing. Make no more rules, limitations, or procedures than absolutely necessary for the functioning of the system. But make sure you specify enough structure to make the design clear and precise. Design by specifying the essential structure, the 'what,' and leave the 'how' to the people who will live with it.

I recently worked with a senior manager who was preparing his organisation for workplace design. I asked if he had any limitations, any boundaries not open for people to redesign. He replied, 'I don't want people "messing" with personnel issues.' At first I was surprised at this limitation, so I probed. 'What specifically is there about personnel that you don't want people to change?' He thought for a moment and said, 'I don't want teams hiring new workers.' I pushed back, 'Is there some part of the hiring process that teams could be trusted to manage themselves?' After several more go arounds of probing questions, the manager sighed, 'Now that I think about it more clearly, I guess there really isn't any part of the hiring process teams could not be responsible for managing, as long as they follow the law and company policies.' As I explored more deeply into the manager's concerns, it became clear that his minimum critical specification was that any new design be consistent with the law and government regulations. The process of thinking through management boundaries and limitations often results in specifications just like this one that are truly minimum, not saying any more than necessary, and critical, drawing the line of what's open and closed to change.

In order to be truly self managing, a system (work group or organisation) needs the elbow room to control its own goals and processes. Minimum critical specification is a guide for determining what level of self management can be left to the system to control. In designing organisations, don't specify any more than necessary about the design; leave it to the actual work groups to do. Every work group needs room to create their own way of working, and that way of working should allow elbow room for each member to be respected as an individual.

Preparing the workforce. Workplace design workshops work best when all workers participate. If full participation is not possible, make sure everyone has an opportunity to affect the

85

Chapter 7
Getting the
Conditions
right for
Workplace
Design

design. The criteria for proper preparation of the workforce are that when the workshops begin no one is surprised – everyone knows what to expect in the process.

Begin by fully briefing supervisors before starting design workshops. Typically, the supervisory level does not exist in a self managing workplace. It is important that supervisors have worthwhile work to do in the new design. They should be able to optimise their needs for being productive members of the organisation, their six criteria, just as much as line workers. Management should help supervisors explore possible options for their desirable future. Supervisors may want to become team members, or start up a technical resource group. Before the workshops begin, management should guarantee that there will be no forced reductions as a direct result of changing to self management. Supervisors should also not lose pay either. In a large unit, several ex-supervisors and specialists may become a self managing resource group for the organisation, as long as they are no longer in the chain of command when it comes to responsibility for the group's output.

All workers are thoroughly briefed before starting design workshops. The briefing includes: a presentation of design principles; information about the present structure of the organisation; the reasons for changing to self management; minimum critical specifications that guide the design process; and a statement of commitment from management. Workers are also briefed on the activities in the workshops. Readiness boils down to knowledge of the design principles and information about the process. When people walk into the room to start the design process, they should not be surprised by anything. Everyone knows why they are there and what they are going to do.

Management can join in the design process. They can kick off participative design workshops by communicating their minimum critical specifications, encouragement, and commitment to the change. Management can be present at the end of workshops, as well, to hear the organisational implications of design features, such as training requirements. Remember, management will then have its own participative design workshop to redesign its work.

Many organisations add another preparation step – stakeholder analysis. People who make the products or deliver the services often are not fully aware of their business environment. It is useful to assess the needs of the organisation's stakeholders, either before the design workshops or as an added activity in the workshop,

We call everyone in your organisation's environment stakeholders. We call them stakeholders because they have an impact on the success of the organisation. They have a stake in your future. Start the assessment of your external environment by scanning your organisation's immediate business and social environment. Brainstorm what's changing in your environment. Examples might be: specific changes in organisational strategy; a new mission for your organisation; a change in government regulation; social changes that affect the nature of your product or service.

Then identify the most important changes in your environment and analyse what they mean to the success of your organisation. Decide what impact these changes have on your organisation. Next, do a stakeholder map. Start by identifying the stakeholders who are important to your team's success. Stakeholders could be people, teams, or organisations. They could be other functions in your larger company, such as marketing or research and development. Remember, executive management might also be an important stakeholder for you.

Answer the following questions for each stakeholder. You can do this activity with the stakeholder in the room working with you. Both you and the stakeholder will learn much about your mutual relationship.

Chapter 7
Getting the
Conditions
right for
Workplace
Design

1. What does the stakeholder provide for our organisation? What do we provide for the stockholder?

2. What expectations and requirements does the stakeholder have for us? What expectations and requirements do we have for the stakeholder?

3. How are we meeting each other's expectations and requirements today? How will these expectations and requirements change in the future?

4. What changes or improvements do we need to make for us to meet each other's expectations and requirements?

5. Should we be challenging each other's expectations and requirements, and if so, how?

After interviewing all your stakeholders, take the information you have gathered and discuss what it means for redesigning your workplace.

Designing the workshops. We have seen many creative and adaptive ways organisations have used to do design workshops. In this book you will read stories about organisations that took a capacity building route to workplace design. They brought in consultants experienced in doing workplace design workshops to train people in their own organisation to do the workshops themselves. The advantage of this capacity building strategy is that a core of people with self management knowledge remains after the design process is finished and the experts have gone home.

We also know of a small group of court reporters who did the participative design workshop on themselves. The supervisor of the section had resigned, leaving a void. The staff approached management and got permission to explore becoming a self managing group. Using the material in the participative design workshop chapter of this book, the court reporters worked through the steps in their spare time and decided to be self managing, and not to replace their supervisor.

Regardless of whether you bring in consultants, use a capacity building approach, or do-it-yourself, there are many ways to design the process. Doing workplace design does not require degrees of higher education in management theory, or extensive training in facilitation of groups.

For a small well defined workplace, like a bank or school, everybody can work together on the design. An example is the Land Bank of South Africa discussed earlier in the book. In larger organisations everyone can also participate, but this time in a series of workplace design workshops.

The generic workshop design we use for larger organisations looks like this. Each workshop consists of a deep slice of the overall workplace. (A 'deep slice' means people from different levels of the hierarchy and different work functions across the organisation.) People form small design teams of 6-8 members each. Each design team is also a deep slice of the whole organisation being redesigned. This produces an overall workshop of 24-32 members, a group size large enough for diverse perspectives, and small enough to allow for face to face decision making. The four design teams work through the six criteria and skill assessment activities, then each does a redesign of the whole organisation. The four designs are reconciled, producing a final design. This workshop design takes about two days per workshop. You can do a series of these deep slice workshops until everyone has participated. Then the various design options are sorted out and a final one is approved by the whole organisation either in a vote or large group process.

Once a final design is agreed upon, then new work groups are formed. The new self managing work groups use the 'Practicalities' activities in the participative design workshop as a guide for getting started. They can also use the chapter in this book, 'A Start Up Guide for Self Managing Teams.' It is critical that new teams define their structure and clearly lay out their work processes. The bureaucratic practices of the past need to be replaced with well defined participative procedures. Otherwise, there is a danger of drifting into laissez faire and apathy.

After the final workplace design is determined, ex-supervisors have their own design workshops to design themselves into support teams, or find other valuable work to do. Also, middle and top managers do design workshops to design their new management work. Self managing workplace design is for everyone in the organisation, including management. Workers need to understand that self management is the structure of the

Chapter 7
Getting the
Conditions
right for
Workplace
Design

whole workplace, not just teams at the bottom of the hierarchy. This is the only way real structural change will happen and be sustainable.

The Grassroots Approach

We have learned some valuable lessons from modern architectural principles. From architecture, we know that grand master plans are not the way to build anything, not a town, a building, or even an organisation. The grand master plan results in heavy, monolithic, autocratic structures. It produces a sterile uniformity. Grand visions are weighty and easily turned into rigid power structures.

A popular metaphor used in many organisational change programs is the 'cascade.' It starts with top management developing a vision and a change process. The grand plan is often based on the training of all workers. Reward and communication systems are put in place to reinforce the desired change. Then the cascade of training and change goes down the hierarchy. The metaphor is elegant, unless you have ever stepped into a real cascade in nature. It's dangerous; a person could get killed. And, of course, cascading grand plans frequently fail when people step into them. Who would voluntarily walk into a cascade? One of the original cascading grand plans was developed by Lenin, I think, and implemented by Stalin.

Russians have a way of thinking about change that is communicated in this quotation from sociologist Tatyana Zaslavskaya. '[Change] is like a spring bursting from the rocks in this mountainside of ours. It comes from an underground stream flowing somewhere beneath the surface of the soil.'[2] The self managing workplace needs to bubble up, not be forced down. Follow the philosophy of manageable steps, a grassroots approach. This is a philosophy by which a structure (building or organisation) can grow in an evolutionary way to achieve the needs of its occupants. It's a grass roots approach and has three characteristics:

- ◆ A set of shared design principles governing evolutionary growth and change;
- ◆ A philosophy of piecemeal development;
- ◆ Local control of design by those who will occupy the space.

In the context of self managing workplace design, self management guides the redesign effort and sets in motion new patterns of behaviour in the workplace. For democratic structure to take hold in a workplace, people at all levels and in every part of a system need to embrace self management knowingly and willingly, top to bottom.

Piecemeal steps means changing from bureaucratic to self management in one part of the organisation at a time. What form self management takes depends on design decisions made at the local level, where people occupy the space. Once the change to self management has occurred, then changes to everything from pay systems to technology follow. Once self management has taken root in the workplace, people will naturally improve their technical work systems and look towards new pay and reward systems that fit their new design.

For example, a big company with several thousand people, many divisions, and separate sites started redesign with management commitment to self management at the top. Then, each local unit of the company redesigned itself using self management, determining the design that was best at their local level.

When designing a workplace, shared design principles guide the change process. When we apply this philosophy to organisation design, we can build workplaces that respect shared principles, retain a harmony of vision throughout, but not a dull uniformity. These kinds of workplaces are full of energy, places where human beings continuously breathe life into their designs. The American historian, Howard Zinn, made this observation about social change: 'Revolutionary change does not come as one cataclysmic moment (beware of such moments!) but as an endless succession of surprises, moving zigzag towards a more decent society. Small acts, when multiplied by millions of people, can transform the world.'[3]

Chapter 7
Getting the
Conditions
right for
Workplace
Design

Making Parts Whole

Here's a thought from architect Christopher Alexander on building: 'In nature, a thing is always born, and developed, as a whole. [Design] is not a sequence of adding parts together, but a whole which expands, crinkles, differentiates itself. Nothing alive can be built by putting preformed parts together.'[4] Self management means building the whole back into parts. It's a matter of repairing the damage of treating people as replaceable parts.

Making parts whole needs to happen at every level of any workplace. If we consider the work group as the part we are building, then we design so that all the skills and abilities needed to deliver the product or service are contained within the group itself. At the level of the individual worker, building the whole into the part means providing each person with the opportunity to do a whole job, including making decisions about the work itself. But be careful here. Organisations have made the mistake over the years of thinking that job enrichment and cross training alone will do the trick. We now know that people become whole in their work when they have a democratic group structure. A self managing workplace is one in which every person is encouraged and supported to reach their highest potential. I once saw a poster in an office where the team concept was all the rage. It said, 'There is no "I" in the word team.' The point being made, I suppose, is that effective teams sublimate the needs and desires of the individual. Nothing could be further from the truth. The most powerful work systems are ones built on differences, with a common sense of purpose and direction, and plenty of elbow room for people within it to follow their individual goals.

Even a small organisation, like a factory or service centre, can be seen as a part, a small cog, in a larger organisation. Making any organisational unit whole means locating responsibility within that unit, and designing it so that it has the internal capacity to provide a complete product or service. An example is a large state agency that used the design principle of self management to relocate responsibility from central administration to the

field. Or consider the major retail department store chain that
restructured its stores within each region so that each store
became a self managing unit.

You can even apply the principles to countries. The most
noteworthy bureaucratic designer of this century was Stalin. He
designed the Soviet Union so that decisions went through
Moscow. He considered every republic to be a replaceable part,
a cog in the Soviet machine. In order to build a tractor, goals
were controlled in Moscow. Engine parts were made in the
Ukraine, tires in Uzbekistan, steering wheels in Siberia, and so
on. As a result, no single republic could be self sustaining.
Trying to build wholes into each republic is proving to be a
formidable challenge for the former Soviet republics.

Chapter 7
Getting the
Conditions
right for
Workplace
Design

Chapter 8

A Start Up Guide For Self Managing Teams

The purpose of this guide[1] is to help your new self managing team get off to the best possible start. The guide addresses the important organising tasks facing any new work team. The best way to use this guide is as a tool for organising your team during the first months of its existence.

This Start Up Guide is designed to complement the participative design workshops your organisation used for workplace redesign. The guide works for teams in any kind of organisation – business, government, or not for profit. It can be used by people on the shop floor, professionals, research and development specialists, managers, and project teams – anywhere people need to organise themselves to get work done.

Your team can decide the best way to use the guide. Use it in a 'do-it-yourself' way. You can start at any point, or work through it from beginning to end. Your team can complete all the tasks at one time, or set up meetings weekly to do different tasks. Find the variation that works best for your team. The important thing is to do all the tasks in the guide fully within the first month or two and then review each task regularly, making changes when necessary.

Keep in mind that team design is never really finished. Just when you think you have your team organised just right, something changes. Maybe new people join the team, or the nature of your product or service changes, or market changes lead to a different level of production requirements. And once you start out as a self managing team, you will find that you will continue to want to develop to higher levels of self management.

So keep this guide after you have finished going through the tasks the first time. You will need to review your progress from time to time, and the tasks that follow will serve you well into the future.

What Is A Self Managing Team?

A self managing team is a group of people who are responsible for the control and coordination of their own work.

There are four kinds of self managing teams:

1. Multi-skilled teams. Multi-skilled means that people in the group do a variety of tasks and functions. They work in a self managing team that has the wherewithal to provide coverage to make sure all tasks, technical and managerial, are performed.

2. Teams that are self managing, but not multi-skilled. In this kind of team, members have different skills and knowledge, allowing them to specialise in a profession or technology. In some research and development organisations, for example, teams are made up of people with such diverse skills as chemistry, marketing, and engineering. It makes no sense for a chemist to learn engineering skills. But it does make sense for this kind of team to take responsibility for coordinating its work together.

3. Project teams. Project teams are temporary self managing teams that come together to do a time bounded task. Their lifetime could vary from several weeks to many months. An example is a team that comes together to fix a complex technical problem or develop new software programs.

4. Management Teams. Managers form self managing teams, too. These are either middle or top management teams. These teams are self managing because managers control and co-ordinate their own work. This is different from the traditional organisation in which managers control and coordinate the work of others below them.

Top management teams are responsible for shaping the organisation's strategy and direction. They also develop ongoing relations with the environment of the organisation, attending to regulatory concerns, stakeholder expectations, and changes in the competitive environment. Middle management teams are responsible for integration across the organisation's boundaries, and they negotiate goals with other self managing teams.

Self managing teams do not ordinarily have supervisors who are responsible for team performance and leadership. Nor does a self managing team have a supervisor who has a changed role to facilitator, coach, or leader, but is still responsible for the team.

What Do Self Managing Teams Control and Coordinate?

Your team is self managing, but is *not* autonomous. Your team is working with materials and equipment belonging to the larger organisation. You are working in conditions where the organisation, not your team, is responsible for strategy, pay rates, and attention to regulatory concerns. So being a self managing team does not mean you can do whatever you want. It's not laissez faire, or anything goes. Self management means your team is responsible for its own work and cooperates with other teams to make the organisation successful.

Here are some of the things self managing teams can control and coordinate:

♦ Assign their members to daily work tasks
♦ Set and monitor production or service goals
♦ Schedule service delivery and production runs
♦ Monitor and measure the productivity and quality of their work

- ◆ Manage vacation and sick leave for its members
- ◆ Maintain good customer and stakeholder relationships
- ◆ Select, review, and discipline its own members
- ◆ Coordinate and conduct training and development of team members
- ◆ Maintain coordinated relationships with other teams and management

Teams decide for themselves what level of self management they will take responsibility for, and negotiate this with management. For example, some self managing teams are comfortable starting out with responsibility for interviewing new team members, but not for disciplining members who are not performing.

Some self managing teams take on some budget responsibility at the beginning, others do not. Many self managing teams evolve into doing performance reviews, preferring to start out with other responsibilities. Your team chooses the level of self management that is right for you, and then negotiates this with management.

Principles of Self management

There are two principles that are important for your team to understand if you are going to develop to higher levels of self management over the coming months and years.

The design principle of self management. The design principle of self management says: *Locate responsibility for control and coordination of work with the people who do the work.*

This design principle is like the DNA, the genetic code or building block, from which your team and organisation can develop. The basic building block of the self managing workplace is the self managing team.

The reason your organisation decided to change to self management is to improve productivity and quality through its people. When people have workplaces where they can make decisions, set goals, support one another on teams, see the whole product from beginning to end, and have a future worth working for, they do productive work.

Self management is not a rigid rule, but a completely different way of designing a workplace. In the bureaucratic workplace, the principle is different: responsibility for the control and coordination of work is located at least one level above where the work occurs.

Open Systems Thinking. Open systems is a principle that can guide the behaviour of your team. The principle says, *Any system to survive and prosper must have an open and direct relationship with its environment.*

We use the term 'system' to mean any organisation, community, or team that draws a boundary around itself to establish its relationship to its environment. 'Environment' means everything outside the system.

Your team is a new social system just now coming to life. Your team's environment is fast changing and demanding. Your environment includes all the other self managing teams in your organisation, management teams, and customers and suppliers – inside and outside your organisation. Your environment is also made up of all those people and forces outside your team's larger organisation that have an impact on the success of your work – competitors, government regulators, local community groups, just to name a few. Even changes in the larger global society affect your team.

It is important that your new team is constantly aware of what's happening in its external environment. Your team will be successful if you develop and maintain strong positive relationships with people and groups in and outside your organisation. Remember to stay aware of what's changing around you.

Task 1 – Team Boundaries: Decisions and Tasks Belonging to Your Team

Self managing teams need clear boundaries defining what the team can and cannot control and coordinate. Boundaries are limits to the area of responsibility of the team.

For example, there are some 'givens' such as organisation policies, government laws and regulations, and union contract limitations that your team cannot ignore. No team can decide for itself to ignore a law or regulation, or change the specifications the customer expects to see on the product or service they are buying.

So, identifying your team's boundaries helps you understand what decisions you can make, and which decisions need to be negotiated with management or others in the organisation. Decisions may include production schedules and goals, hiring new team members, as well as assignments of team members to daily jobs.

You also need to identify tasks that belong to the team. Tasks are the work activities your team performs every day to get the product out the door or the service delivered to a customer.

Make the following lists to identify your team's boundaries:

- ♦ Decisions and tasks completely owned by the team;
- ♦ Areas outside the team's control, such as legal obligations, organisation policy, or union contract;
- ♦ Decisions and tasks shared between the team and management, and other teams;
- ♦ Decisions the team is consulted on, but *not* responsible for making.

You can do this list activity with management in the room, or negotiate it with them later. Understand that management will do the same activity to be clear about their own boundaries. So you can expect some interesting discussions when you compare your lists.

Task 2 – Team Goals

Team goals answer the question, 'What is the purpose of this team?' Goals keep teams focused on what's important, the reason the team exists. Goals also help teams continue to develop and learn on the job. Without setting its own goals, no team can be self managing. There are three kinds of goals:

- ◆ Team production or service goals that focus the team on its output
- ◆ Team development goals that encourage the team to keep improving itself
- ◆ Individual development goals for each team member's desirable future

Here's a team production goal from a hospital human resources group: *We will process requisitions for new job postings within 24 hours of receipt.*

A team goal example from a hi-tech manufacturing workplace: *We will produce 20 computer units per day at 100% quality.*

Production and service goals measure the work output of the team – the number and quality of the product or service.

Development goals measure team growth and development over time. A team development goal example: *0 injuries on the job this quarter.*

Individual goals help each team member realise their desirable future at work. Individual goal example: *Team member Mary will improve her leadership skills by serving as the team's contact person during the next three months.*

Begin goal setting by agreeing on a few (3-6) key production or service goals for the team. Make sure each goal is specific, clear, and that it has a time and quality expectation. Negotiate these goals with management. Remember, management might have different expectations from your team. Negotiating means listening, discussing, and being ready to compromise.

Then move on to team development goals and individual goals. Remember, in the area of individual goals, the strategy is to provide each team member with a good job and a desirable future at work. But this doesn't necessarily mean anyone can do what they want. Your team needs to always balance the desires of the individual team member with the overall goals and available resources of the team.

People
In
Charge

Task 3 – Team Ground Rules

Self managing teams are most effective when they agree on ground rules for behaviour.

In team meetings, for example, it may be useful to have ground rules that keep the team focused on its task, respecting the participation of all members.

A more general team ground rule might be: *Arrange for someone to cover for you when you have a scheduled day off.*

This kind of ground rule can help the team manage its consistency.

Your self managing team should pay attention to developing specific team ground rules for managing conflict among its members. In traditional, bureaucratic workplaces, supervisors take care of conflicts and disagreements among workers. Now it is up to team members to manage their own conflict.

Be careful setting ground rules. There is a tendency sometimes to make a rule for every problem. Often rules are made to address a problem instead of dealing with the person who had the problem. Rule making can be a way of avoiding conflicts.

Use the principle of minimum critical specification as your guide. Minimum critical specification means specifying only what is essential to make your team self managing.

Make no more rules, limitations, or procedures than absolutely necessary for the functioning of your team.

Task 4 – Team Information Systems

Self managing teams need timely, accurate feedback so they know the results of their work. Feedback is information from people, like customers, or from technologies that tell us how we did – mistakes and successes.

Feedback is timely and accurate when it comes directly to the team from the source of the problem, that part of the work process where and when the problem occurred.

Feedback and information systems allow self managing teams to measure their own effectiveness so they know how they are performing against their production or service goals.

Self managing teams need to develop information management systems that help them coordinate their work. Self managing teams require open, explicit documentation of goals, methods, and responsibilities. Typically, effective self managing teams have charts, graphs, and schedules posted publicly on walls for all to see, or on computer programs and E-mail.

These are some of the key questions to answer as your team develops its information plan:

♦ What results do you need to measure?

♦ What information do you need to have in order to measure results of your team's work?

♦ Who has this information now?

♦ How and in what form should this information be gathered?

♦ What systems or processes do you need to put into place to gather and analyse information?

♦ What documentation and publication methods will you use to communicate the results of your team's work? Wall charts, E-mail, etc.

Task 5 – Team Coordination

A team that is well coordinated is a team that has everything and everyone working together, aligned in the same direction, towards the accomplishment of its goals, as well as the overall goals of the organisation.

A person who is coordinated is someone whose parts – mind and body – work together. We joke about some people: 'He can't walk and chew gum at the same time.' We say that a person who is a good coordinator is one who can keep many balls in the air at the same time – a good juggler of complex tasks and functions. It's the same with a team.

In traditional bureaucratic workplaces we depend on the supervisor to handle work coordination. In self managing teams, everyone takes the lead at different times in providing coordination.

Team coordination tasks might include:

♦ Keeping supplies flowing to the team
♦ Monitoring feedback systems
♦ Representing the team at organisation meetings
♦ Being the point of contact between the team and other teams and parts of the organisation
♦ Passing important information across shifts
♦ Being the point of contact for the team when a member is sick or needs help

A self managing team identifies the tasks it needs to coordinate and decides how to best make sure this coordination is done. The team may either develop coordination systems, or rotate coordinating tasks among its members, so everyone can become skilled, and so that no one person is overburdened with too much responsibility.

Self managing teams don't have leaders appointed by management. Nor do self managing teams select permanent leaders from their own ranks. Having permanent leaders results in the same kind of problems you had in the bureaucratic organisation. The boss made the decisions, controlling and coordinating your work.

Here are some tasks to help your team ensure its effective coordination:

1 Identify the coordination tasks your team needs to address;

2. Decide how the team will coordinate these tasks – whether a system can be put in place, or a person should be assigned to coordinate that function;

3. Then have individual team members take the first turn at being coordinator for each task you identified.

It's important to put a time limit on how long each person will perform their coordinating task. Make it long enough so people in other parts of the organisation or customers experience regularity. Make it short enough that it is not seen as a permanent position of authority.

Self managing teams maintain a skills matrix to track the skill development of its members, and to plan for the skill development of the team. The skills matrix is a barometer telling the team how deep and broad its skills are.

To make a skills matrix, start by identifying all the skills and technical knowledge required to get the work of the team done. On a matrix, list these skills as shown in the example matrix below. Place each team member's name across the top. Then compile a collective picture of your team's skill resources by using a simple scale:

- *0* for none of a particular skill
- One tick ✔ for a sufficient level of skill
- Two ticks ✔✔ for high level of skill, meaning this person could teach the skill to others

Example Matrix:

ESSENTIAL SKILLS	NANCY	TOM	MARTIN	STEPHANIE	GARY
A	✔✔	✔	0	0	0
B	✔	✔	✔	✔	✔✔
C	0	✔✔	✔✔	0	✔
D	✔	✔✔	✔✔	0	0
E	✔	✔✔	✔	0	✔
F, etc.					

The matrix can point out team skill deficiencies and opportunities for training members so there is more back-up on the team.

Your team should use your matrix to develop a team skill development plan. Your plan specifies what training people on the team need to make sure the team meets its goals.

Consider the following questions when doing your team plan:

♦ Identify the strengths and weaknesses of your team. Where are you underskilled?

♦ How much back-up skill does your team require to ensure getting its work done in a way that meets your team goals?

♦ Who needs training in what? List names of team members and what training they need.

♦ Where do you get the training? Can someone on the team do it, or should you go to an outside resource? How much will it cost, and how do you pay for it?

Task 7 – Managing and Improving Your Team's Work Processes

Self managing teams own their work processes and are responsible for continuously solving problems and improving the work system.

Completing the following tasks will improve your team's work system.

1. Draw a diagram of your current work processes on chart paper so everyone has a clear understanding of how work moves through the team, from beginning to end. Work processes start with inputs to the team, like raw materials and customer orders, and end with outputs such as products or services.

2. Brainstorm the process problems that occur in your current work flow. Process problems are any deviation from a quality standard, a malfunction, delay, foul-up, breakdown, or unplanned event that has a negative impact on schedule, quality, or cost.

3. Prioritise your list of process problems, using criteria like impact on quality, cost, or customer satisfaction.

4. When you have identified the key problems, answer these questions for each one:

    ♦ What's the technical problem?
    ♦ What's the impact?
    ♦ What are the causes?
    ♦ How is the problem handled now, and by whom?
    ♦ How might the problem be solved or prevented?

5. Develop an action plan for responding to each key problem. Include: a clear description of the problem, your plan for solving or preventing it, and identification of who will work on it and when. Your plan may require fixing the problem or completely redoing the process.

Here's another way to do this activity. Instead of drawing your team's work process on paper, bring your process to life by simulating what happens step by step. This is particularly useful for teams that are made up of people coming from different parts of the process.

For example, a new team in a court system literally passed a case file around from team member to member to demonstrate what happens in the process beginning to end. Another example is a new marketing team made up of people from different functions related to marketing and sales. They had a person role play what happens to a customer as they are passed around the parts of the marketing process.

As a new team, you may find that you need to invent new work processes, or start from scratch because the old process is too broken to fix. This requires a 'clean sheet' approach in which your team maps out on chart paper each step in a new process, noting work activities and decision points along the way. You can start this process mapping by identifying the end product first. Start with the customer or stakeholder expectations for a quality product or service, then go back and identify each step to get there.

Regularly review changes and problems that occur in your team's work flow. It's the job of your team to constantly monitor and improve your process so that you can achieve your performance goals and be an effective team.

Task 8 – Team Work Space and Equipment Needs

Your self managing team may require some changes in the physical layout of your work space and additional equipment. Self managing teams require:

- ◆ Face to face communication
- ◆ Opportunity for people to be in close physical proximity (if possible)
- ◆ A work space that has room for private work and team meetings

Work spaces in self managing organisations are not set up according to status or hierarchy as they were in the bureaucratic, traditional organisation.

Do the following assessment:

1. Do a current inventory of all equipment, tools, technologies, and work spaces available to the team;

2. Brainstorm ideas for what work space and equipment to keep, get rid of, and add to make sure the team has the resources it needs;

3. Choose those work space changes and equipment needs that are the highest priorities for your team;

4. Develop cost assessments and justify resource needs.

Present your suggestions to management and negotiate for what your team needs. Remember, every other new team is doing the same task. This task requires patience and co-operation with other teams.

Task 9 – Becoming An Open Systems Team

For a team to become an open system team, it has to develop open and direct relationships with its external environment. The external environment is everyone and everything outside your team's boundary, including management, other teams, people who supply your team, and customers who use your products or services. The external environment also includes changes and trends in your team's larger organisation, the industry, local community, and society at large.

Start the assessment of your external environment by scanning your team's immediate business and social environment. Brainstorm things changing in your environment. Examples might be: specific changes in organisational strategy; a new mission for your organisation; a change in government regulation; social changes that affect the nature of your product or service.

Then identify the most important changes in your environment and analyse what they mean to the success of your team. Decide what to do about them so you are contributing to the overall success of the team and the rest of the organisation.

Next, do a stakeholder analysis. We call everyone in your team's environment stakeholders. We call them stakeholders because they have an impact on you and are important to your success. They have a stake in your future.

Start by identifying the stakeholders who are important to your team's success. Stakeholders could be people, teams, or organisations. Remember that management is also an important stakeholder for your team. Be sure to discuss your mutual expectations with them.

Answer the following questions for each stakeholder. You can do this activity with the stakeholder in the room working with you. Both you and the stakeholder will learn much about your mutual relationship.

1. What does the stakeholder provide for our team? What does our team provide for the stockholder?

2. What expectations and requirements does the stakeholder have for our team? What expectations and requirements do we have for the stakeholder?

3. How are we meeting each other's expectations and requirements today? How will these expectations and requirements change in the future?

4. What changes or improvements do we need to make for us to meet each other's expectations and requirements?

5. Should we be challenging each other's expectations and requirements, and if so, how?

113

Chapter 8
A Start Up
Guide for
Self Managing
Teams

After interviewing all your stakeholders, take the information you have gathered and discuss what it means to your team. How does this new information affect your team goals, relationships with stakeholders, the processes you use to do your work? Make changes in your work systems to meet, and maybe even exceed, the expectations of your stakeholders.

Review these questions regularly with your important stakeholders. You will find that your team will become more effective as it develops positive working relationships with all its stakeholders.

Task 10 – Review the Six Criteria for Productive Work

A self managing team has a goal of providing its members with a good job. A good job is one that satisfies each person's needs to be a productive person. Over time, your team can measure its development by periodically assessing each member's satisfaction.

The following six basic human requirements must be present on your team for people to be productive. These human requirements are a foundation for designing an effective team. They are so important that we call them the six criteria for productive work. These needs are experienced to different degrees in different people. The six criteria are:

1. Elbow Room for Decision Making. People need to feel that they are their own bosses and that, except in exceptional circumstances, they have room to make decisions they can call their own. On the other hand, they do not need so much elbow room that they just do not know what to do.

2. Opportunity to Learn On the Job and Go On Learning. Learning is a basic human need and activity. Learning is possible only when people are able to:
 a) Set goals that are reasonable challenges for them, and
 b) Get feedback of results in time for them to correct their behaviour.

3. Variety. People need to be able to vary their work to avoid the extremes of boredom and fatigue. They need to set up a satisfying rhythm of work that provides enough variety and a reasonable challenge.

4. Mutual Support and Respect. People need to be able to get help and respect from their co-workers.

5. Meaningfulness. People need to be able to relate what they do and what they produce to their social life. Meaningfulness includes both the worth and quality of a product, and having a knowledge of the whole product. Many jobs lack meaning because workers see only such a small part of the final product that its meaning is denied them. Meaningfulness has two dimensions:
a) Socially useful,
and
b) Seeing the whole product.

115

Chapter 8
A Start Up
Guide for
Self Managing
Teams

Taken together, these dimensions make it possible for a person to see a real connection between their daily work and the world.

6. A Desirable Future. Put simply, people need a job that leads to a desirable future for themselves, not a dead end. This desirable future is not necessarily a promotion, but a career path that will continue to allow personal growth and increase in skills.

Your team can complete its own six criteria matrix. Construct a matrix on a flip chart.

Put the names of your team members along the top, and the six criteria down the side. Starting with the first item – elbow room – discuss how much elbow room each team member is currently experiencing in the team. Put a score down for each person. Discuss and score the rest of the six items, using the following scoring instruction.

Because the first three criteria need to be optimal for each individual, these three are scored from -5 (too little) to +5 (too much), with 0 being optimal, just right.

As the second three criteria are things you can never have too much of, they are scored from 0 (none) to 10 (lots).

The final group product will express the range of scores across the section. It is best to do this activity as a group task. Everyone in the group discusses their own scores as they see them. They share their perceptions of others scores, discussing and negotiating differences in perceptions, changing their scores if necessary, and arriving collectively at a picture of how their team meets their needs.

Review all the scores on the matrix and develop a plan for improving the satisfaction levels of team members where necessary. This is a good learning activity to do every 36 months as a reality check to make sure everyone on your team has worthwhile work.

People
In
Charge

Continuous Learning and Development

Once your team completes all the start up tasks in this guide, you are well on the road to self management. Remember, your team will continue to develop and evolve over the months and years ahead. The overall goal is for your organisation to become increasingly successful because of the participation of its people. In the process, each member of your team strives toward their desirable future at work.

Your team's level of self management will not grow by accident. It will take hard work and diligence on the part of the whole team. Keep reviewing these 10 tasks on a regular basis, at least every three months, making changes as you go forward. Team learning and development require a good balance of action and reflection. Get in the habit of regularly taking time out to reflect. Team reflection means to discuss what you have been learning as a team. It also means being critical and demanding of yourselves and the organisation.

People
In
Charge

The next seven chapters are case stories written by managers and consultants involved in workplace redesign. These stories illustrate how several organisations used the ideas in this book to change their structure to self management. They include small and large workplaces from both the private and public sectors. And they come from different parts of the world. The workplaces are a call centre, a winery, the U.S. courts, a chamber music orchestra, a do-it-yourself retail store chain, and a manufacturer of medical instruments – a wide variety of types of organisations.

Chapter 9

Improving Customer Satisfaction at Prudential

Fran Ryan and Clare Connor

This is a story, still unfinished, of the triumph of energy and enthusiasm of frontline staff over the many hurdles that come with being in a rapidly changing and highly regulated servicing environment. The setting is a call centre with 200 staff, part of the Life and Pensions business within Prudential. Staff here look after calls from about 7,000 of our customers and sales staff every day. Typically the calls are about the pensions products the customer has bought from one of our Direct Sales Consultants.

Back in summer of 1998, the call centre itself was struggling under the weight of huge volumes of incoming calls, making it almost impossible to take time out for anything, (even a day to do the design work we'd need). There was a terrific imperative to reduce costs which has increased since then with the advent of new government regulated low cost products; and added to that there was a history of relentless but piecemeal 'improvement' initiatives of which this must have seemed to be yet another.

As well as pressures from the immediate environment, it was difficult to see how the work of a teleconsultant could be significantly changed to make it more satisfying. There was zero discretion around changing the system (a relatively new work flow and image system had been introduced which enabled big productivity gains but changing it would have been impossible), and on the face of it the work looked simple and repetitive.

The project itself was introduced from the middle rather than the top, never an ideal place to start, and got the green light more out of a sense of 'nothing to lose' than a positive sense that self management was the right place to go. The story, however, illustrates the robustness of this methodology even in an arena fraught with difficulties. It is still early days and this is very much a report of work in progress, but already there is a distinct feeling of promise.

Background

Call centres are frequently referred to as the 'sweatshop of the nineties' due to their strict regime where staff have their working hours, breaks and lunches scheduled in advance and are continuously monitored by advanced telephony and MI systems. Typically, large call centres, will have upwards of two hundred staff, with row after row of individuals, the majority of whom are female, literally wired to their telephones and computers, all wearing headsets so hands are free to type. However, if you took a walk through our call centres, you'd be impressed with the busy buzz of purposeful animated conversation, as 200 teleconsultants wield their 7,000 calls a day with some of our 6 million customers who are ringing up from all over the UK to find out about their pensions, life or savings policies.

The story really begins with the fact that beneath this apparent aura of buzz and apparent health lay a very serious problem: there was widespread concern about staff attrition rates. This was a problem not only because of the visible cost (by our calculation, a conservative £·5m to cover the cost of replacing staff in the previous 12 months) but also because of the effect on the bottom line: customer service and retention.

Fran is an organisational psychologist and with ten years experience of organisation design and development, including recruitment and retention, she believed that lack of autonomy

121

Chapter 9
Improving
Customer
Satisfaction at
Prudential

and variety were central causes in call centre attrition. But could anything be done about that in a call centre? Had anyone tried? Research revealed no examples. However, there is a large body of published research around the predictors of job satisfaction which in turn predict employee retention. If employees don't have sufficient autonomy (and some other things as well) they are not satisfied at work. If not satisfied they tend to leave, and are certainly not as productive as satisfied staff. All of which leads to poor customer service, poor customer retention, poor or zero profit and a moribund organisation.

But Fran had an approach that she believed would work: the participative design workshop. This is the only methodology we came across that directly tackles the issue of job satisfaction, which in our case (and in any service organisation) is so crucially linked to customer satisfaction. However there were a number of questions to address before getting to the starting blocks:

♦ Would the leadership team support the approach? How would it fit within a traditional structure?

♦ Was a self managing team based approach the right one?

♦ How could we get staff released to do the workshop? What budget, support, training would be needed?

♦ Where would it be best to start?

♦ How would this approach work in a call centre as there is little or no control over incoming work?

Getting leadership support

This was the most important starting point and, from our position at the time, it also presented quite a challenge. The Prudential has thrived on a traditional hierarchical arrangement for over 150 years. Moving toward self management and especially using the participative design approach explicitly sets out to give control and coordination of work to the teams doing the work. This seemed to be a tough step for the leadership to take in this context, especially as there were no guarantees of success.

A couple of other organisation development people, Ros Bailey and Mary Walkland, agreed that the participative design approach might work. They provided the entrée to Julie Deacon, the call centre director, who was very interested. None had Fran's belief or knowledge of the process but as things could hardly get worse, they were interested in trying something that could be more than a short term fix. This approach had the potential to *radically change the culture* and could furthermore build capability for continuously improving customer service and processes into the future. A cynic might say we had little to lose. All were agreed that something needed to happen to radically reinvent the whole culture so staff could really be enabled to put the customer first.

Was a self managed team based approach the right one?

Research on the predictors of job satisfaction and retention suggest several important variables but a crucial and common one, cited in several different places, is autonomy. Given also the needs within the call centre to have a flexible capability to respond quickly to ever-changing customer needs, there seemed little doubt that the existing strongly team based culture would benefit from more self management. While we worried about leadership support, we had no doubt that staff would be very much in favour of self management. There has been quite a lot of press coverage in the UK of the changing nature of the employment contract: employees are no longer expecting 'jobs for life' but are on the other hand expecting to be treated with far greater respect and to be given far greater responsibility. We had anecdotal evidence and some also from staff opinion surveys that staff sometimes felt under utilised and felt they could be better valued for their contribution and given more responsibility.

Grade of service, our primary measure, was low. There were lots of initiatives to try to improve things, so much so that one previous internal survey had already referred to the 'initiativitis' that seemed to have taken hold. The staff were tired, with the sheer volume of calls and the uphill nature of getting out of the negative spiral. As customers waited longer and queues built up, complaints increased which resulted in more call backs. This increased the queue, and the wait, and so on, and things got into a very negative spiral that at times threatened to spin out of control.

How could we get the OK to take more time out of an already depleted workforce to do a participative design workshop? And how would the staff feel about what was, after all, from their perspective yet another initiative?

The director decided to take the plunge but we could only have a day and a half! We grabbed it and left our other questions unanswered. We had an opportunity albeit not an ideal one and as things in the real world of work are almost never ideal, we put all our energy into it!

Design and leadership of the workshop

Next was to sketch out how we would do it. Although trained very comprehensively on two separate occasions, once from the source, as it were, Merrelyn Emery and once by Bob Rehm and Nancy Cebula, Fran wanted to learn more by working with an expert. Nancy Cebula agreed to work in partnership with her. The process looks deceptively simple. The easier bit is running the participative design workshop itself. The more complex elements are how you set it all up and how you follow it through. It also helps, we think, to have the credibility of an external 'expert' when starting something so radically different.

Planning the workshop

People

In

Charge

Who should come? Would we have each team do their own design or somehow arrive at one design for the whole call centre? How much diversity could the call centre handle? After considering several options, the plan emerged as follows:

♦ A one and a half day workshop led by Fran and Nancy with a design team, which would be a cross section of the call centre, to come up with one or two possible designs;

♦ The workshop would include some first line managers whose roles would be changed as a result of the work design;

♦ A follow-up process for getting feedback from those not present;

♦ Feedback integration into one design with design team;

♦ Project plan for pilot, including training and follow-up support, for sign off by the call centre director.

The more usual approach would have been to have each team do their own design and to then consolidate that into a single design for everyone. An alternative would have been to have lots of different teams all with the same goals but all achieving them in their own (probably different) ways.

What's not on the table?

With any approach to organisation and work design it is important to be clear in advance about what is not up for grabs. There were some big things here which needed to be clearly stated up front so as to manage expectation of both staff and leadership:

♦ A sophisticated telephony system combined with a work flow and imaging system had been introduced in the last few years and could not easily be changed. We had to leave it as it was

♦ Key controls to demonstrate compliance with regulatory requirements could not be compromised

♦ Pay could not be changed in the short term

♦ Service levels needed to be maintained

♦ There was to be as little down time as possible throughout both the planning and implementation phases.

Briefing the managers whose work would be affected

This could have been one of the sensitive areas. However, both first and second line call centre managers were aware of the need to do something radical to address the twin problems of staff attrition and customer service. Unexpected support came from two new managers who had had positive experience of self directed work teams. A third set up a visit to another financial services company where success with self managing teams proved a very strong selling point.

Venue booked. Delegates identified. Invitations sent out. Nancy arrives.

The Workshop

This was the most straightforward aspect of the whole pro-gramme. The running order and design are covered in detail elsewhere in this book, but it's worth mentioning a few of the points to give a flavour of what it felt like.

Who came? 19 people including 2 managers, (this is where Clare became involved and subsequently became project manager) two coaches, four technical specialists and 12 teleconsultants represented a good cross section of the call centre. All turned up early at Reading's Victorian Town Hall. The venue was a large assembly room which seemed a suitably awesome place for a programme that we hoped would deliver such a significant cultural shift.

Purpose. The invitations had stated this quite clearly but people still seemed curious but mystified:

- ◆ To improve customer service through improving staff job satisfaction
- ◆ To develop flexibility to respond to constantly changing customer needs
- ◆ If appropriate, to pilot something very different

Design options. Two teams worked in parallel through the design process and came up with two designs that were broadly similar but remained distinct because of two areas where they couldn't agree. The current structure in the call centre was a traditional hierarchical design with director, first and second line managers, and teleconsultants in groups of about twenty. The two new design options emerged because of a particular focus on three of the six criteria – the need for more elbow room, more variety, and a more desirable future.

Both new designs called for self managing teams, each consisting of 10 teleconsultants and a coach. The teams would be responsible for:

127

Chapter 9
Improving
Customer
Satisfaction at
Prudential

♦ Site coverage and scheduling (ensuring there are enough people to cover the phones)
♦ Setting their own goals and targets
♦ Being responsible for achieving their own goals and targets
♦ New entrant development

In the context of the call centre environment, where people have very little control over their work, scheduling becomes a larger than life issue. The idea of people on a team negotiating with each other to determine who works what days and shifts is a powerful display of self management. This is seen by the workers as an indication that management really means what they say about putting responsibility for control and co-ordination of work at the level where the work is done.

The issue of doing quality audits was discussed at length in the workshop. The design team decided that auditing for quality was something the teams could work towards doing for each other over the long term. As people reached a certain level of skill and knowledge they could do quality audits for their team mates. Meanwhile, the coaches would do the audits, listening in to calls randomly, and giving feedback to the teams. But, as the coaches are not above the team in a traditional command and control structure, they act as developmental resources to the teams.

The teams made a wonderful job of presenting to the call centre director at the end, who admitted to being 'gob-smacked' at the breadth and depth of their proposals. She was amazed and a little shocked at the scale of their redesign and was very excited about the energy and creativity shown by the staff. She did a great leadership job in responding positively to their outputs and immediately signing off several areas where people could start work. They all left the room inspired to get on with it.

Even if this design had gone no further, this proved to those assembled beyond any shadow of a doubt that, given the right environment, staff could make a great job of organisation design. No need for expensive external consultants who often get it wrong and have a propensity for generating resistance because of the very 'expertise' they purport to have.

Next Steps

Shortly after the participative design workshop, the design team issued a newsletter to everyone in the call centre. This outlined the process, the results and asked for feedback. When the design team reconvened, all the feedback was consolidated and the differences between the two designs resolved into one. The passage of time seemed to have made this a 'no brainer'.

The final design was then presented to the call centre director for sign off and work began in earnest to decide which teams would pilot the new design and how its success could be measured. Two teams were selected largely because their managers were open and actively supportive of the self managing concept. They were then split into smaller teams of ten to give a balance of skills in each team and these were the teams that then went through a one day implementation workshop. When they were first informed that they would be taking part in the pilot, the idea was received with great enthusiasm. This was encouraging especially to those who had taken part in the design work but were not to be part of the pilot. The full commitment of all involved was seen as crucial to the success of the project.

Concerns about a pilot approach

We had concerns about running a pilot, doing something new in the context of the 'old paradigm' of hierarchy around it. Although we saw ourselves as pioneers with a goal of revolutionising the culture, we still had to work within current organisational tolerance levels and we recognised that we had to start with wherever people were at. So it was a pilot or nothing. That was an easy decision. But would a pilot survive and thrive and win others over or would it be overwhelmed by the sheer weight of pressure? Only time would tell.

Each team within the pilot (only two members had been on the original design workshop), had a one day workshop and a further day's training, after which they fearlessly began their journey into self management!!

The participative design workshop is very different from many approaches that are currently the preserve of aforementioned 'experts': it is a proudly and consciously low-tech approach. All we needed was the workspace, some flip chart paper and pens. These workshops can be run anywhere, (see 'Rebuilding the Land Bank of South Africa') and, unlike some other organisation events we have participated in and even planned, they're not labour intensive before you even start. You don't need an army of people to cover logistics and facilitation. It's small and simple and very people friendly. And it's all about setting up the 'facilitating environment' to borrow a phrase from Winnicott. It's about setting up the environment to encourage the participants to feel they CAN take charge. If they don't do it in the workshop, how will they do it afterwards?

Results

At the end of the first full month we had the first hard measures. It was too little to be certain of, but the trends were excellent. We had expected performance to drop because of the increased amount of idle time being used to perform new responsibilities. It had in fact improved in several areas and was down in only one area.

The noticeable change is in the increase in discretionary effort. This is going into several things, amongst them performance monitoring and improvement. People are sharing ideas and learning from each other, people have an increased sense of ownership and responsibility. The teams are gradually coming to grips with running meetings, dealing with interpersonal conflict and generally dealing with whatever comes their way. In short the culture has changed.

Here's what a few of the staff have said:

One of the managers:

'I'm surprised at how much of my time it's freed up.'

From Teleconsultants:

'Before it was just a job, now we're all really interested in our performance and monitoring it every day.'

'Everyone wants to be a senior teleconsultant as soon as possible.'

'I am now in control more of what happens in my team. This has had a great effect on motivation in my job.'

'Self managing teams have provided me with more variety in my work and job satisfaction. I have more control to improve the way the call centre operates to provide excellent customer service.'

'You get to see things through instead of referring.'

'You are responsible for your own actions, punctuality, etc.'

'Meetings are held on a regular basis to swap ideas and discuss things.'

131

Chapter 9
Improving
Customer
Satisfaction at
Prudential

'It's a good feeling knowing you have more control over what you and your team members can do.'

'We have the ability to deal with performance issues on a more open, almost humorous level, yet achieving very direct results without causing "attitude".'

'At the initial changeover, I found negative feedback from my peer group difficult to swallow. With further team discussion and self expression, we, as a stronger team, have all overcome these obstacles.'

Main areas to 'do better next time' at a recent review were as follows:

Not enough time to prepare, especially to sort out rotating roles and meetings.

Main areas which they are still getting to grips with:

Power sharing
One or two people taking on a more 'managerial' role. This happened in one of the four teams where one person had taken on a particular role and was not rotating it. As this role was a monitoring one, other team members felt that power had become located with one particular person. This had not happened in the other teams where this particular 'monitoring' role was shared by several, if not everyone, on team. All are now working on sorting it out without intervention from outside.

Giving negative feedback
This may be a cultural issue in England! The teams are all finding it tough, learning to give negative feedback. This is in spite of some training. Nonetheless, they are all making headway, are gradually improving, and have identified it as a critical area for further development. We will know we have succeeded in changing culture when we've cracked this one.

Other lessons learned

As we approached the workshop, and even more so immediately afterwards, we noticed several things we might have done better. We learned the hard way that we were under prepared, and now having read many other case studies, under budgeted.

1. Ensure the key people know what they're getting into. Be explicit about the design principles, particularly about the change of locus of control. Although we had got the call centre director to give us the go ahead, wider leadership understanding and alignment was sketchy if there at all. At one point there was a tortured debate about how self managing things were going to be: whether we needed to explicitly discuss moving the locus of control downward. There were huge discussions among the organisation development community about the language: 'bureaucratic' and 'democratic'. Not so with the frontline staff who naturally loved every minute of it, and responded with the most incredible energy, creativity and enthusiasm. We have now evolved a locally intelligible language:

    Design Principle 1: **The Traditional Design Principle;** and
    Design Principle 2: **The Self Managing Design Principle.**

2. Take time to brief the participants fully in advance and at their own pace. Although the participants loved it, they started off being very unsure and we went through several patches of uncertainty and discomfort in the workshop itself. Some of this, but probably not all, would have been offset with better briefing. Recent feedback has suggested that next time we start with a short briefing and issue a one or two page summary of the approach. We follow that at a later stage with a lunch time Q&A session in advance of the first workshop.

3. Brief those who may feel their work may be at risk because of the changes. Another learning was the perceived threat to first line manager roles. This was one group we briefed in advance. Although they themselves seemed to take things in their stride, possibly because we were talking at this point about a small pilot involving about 20% of the total population in the call centre, their staff frequently expressed concern and anxiety about this. This was something we lived with until the managers involved in the pilot became 'converted' and began to preach with such zeal that we didn't need to say a thing. Both pilot managers have become active advocates to introduce the approach to wider groups of employees. Both will be workshop leaders in plans to roll it out to the whole organisation over the next twelve months or so.

4. Call a spade a spade. Be clear about the approach being heavily loaded towards self management. This is no big deal, but in retrospect we may have fudged it a little, as it can appear counter cultural in a traditional organisation. However, as our understanding has grown, we can now see that the approach allows degrees of autonomy and, as the parameters of that autonomy are set at the beginning, the leadership of the organisation is firmly in charge of this.

One of the more interesting questions about this piece of work is the degree to which it is possible to develop self management in a very constrained environment. There are tight systems constraints in the call centre (mentioned above under 'what's not on the table') which reduce the opportunity for autonomy (elbow room); there is little scope for variety as people are physically attached to their telephone and computer. Nonetheless, observation would suggest that people are very inventive and have identified all sorts of things, which they can do and are actively pulling down from management, such as recruitment, and site cover.

5. Prepare for what is to come and plan end to end. Set up follow-up events during or immediately after the design workshop. This can help hold the energy and take it forward. We were waiting for a particular piece of statistical/analytical work to be completed before we called the design team back. This piece of work was delayed and, although a newsletter and feedback questionnaire went out, it was still almost three months (Christmas intervened and call volumes went up) before we got back together again to finalise the design and the plan to take it forward. This wait could have killed the project. It's another point that suggests the robustness of the intervention: staff felt sufficiently strongly and they had understood enough about its significance, and so it survived.

6. Be hands on. Nurturing this kind of thing into life means just that. Although this approach is about self management, the teams need a lot of support through the early days of their work together, particularly to avoid falling back into the trap of looking to one person for the answers. We have four teams in the pilot and each has a dedicated organisation development consultant. Together with the two managers, we are learning about this way of working and consciously building our capability to take it forward to the rest of the organisation. All are working together to ensure that we don't fall into the dependency trap. And striking the right balance is difficult. Too hands on and you destroy the self management; too hands off (laissez faire) and the risk is they fall apart before they get started. Developing an understanding of the need for us to be inactive, sometimes silent, is one of the hardest things we've done, and we're still learning. We are also preparing a whole suite of materials including a workshop for managers whose roles will change because of the gradual roll out of self managing teams.

And finally, as we write, we haven't yet reached the first quarter evaluation, but this approach can already be seen to have delivered important benefits to our business: 40 staff and their two former managers seem to be more satisfied with their work, and believe they are working more effectively. There have been several new initiatives since the pilot started, including the design of a completely new means of measuring customer satisfaction. Already the culture of continuous improvement is emerging. Word is spreading and demand for information and further workshops is growing.

The approach principally enabled staff to give of themselves. There was a huge desire on the part of front line staff to make a real difference, but the situation was one in which the whole structure and process of the call centre had been set up, not consciously, but unconsciously to thwart such good intent. This methodology by its very nature has enabled those same staff at every level to give their best.

135

Chapter 9
Improving
Customer
Satisfaction at
Prudential

Fran Ryan *is an organisational psychologist working in organisation development in Prudential. She is particularly interested in putting people in charge in any environment whether commercial or not for profit, as this seems to be a major route to securing commitment and improving organisational effectiveness.*

E-mail: fran.ryan@prudential.co.uk
fran@ryanmcphail.demon.co.uk

Clare Connor *is a Call Centre Manager working in Prudential.*

E-mail: clare.connor@prudential.co.uk
clare@connor.fsbusiness.co.uk

Both can be contacted at:
Prudential Life and Pensions,
121 King's Road,
Reading,
RG1 3ES, UK

Chapter 10

Making Wine the Self Managing Way At Southcorp

by Bob Baxter

This is the story of how Southcorp's huge Karadoc Winery transformed from a bureaucratic organisation to a self managing workplace. The winery used participative design workshops to redesign into a team based organisation. This story demonstrates how self managing bottling and packaging teams are now taking on former management responsibilities covering safety, quality, process improvement, training, and liaison with other teams. The result is a Karadoc Winery that:

- *Has reduced inventories from 3-4 weeks to 10 days for wine casks and from 2 months to 4-5 weeks for bottled wine;*
- *Dramatically improved safety performance from 1,500 hours lost time a year to less than 80 hours;*
- *Improved productivity across the board annually by 7%.*

The story is told by Bob Baxter, general manager of the Karadoc production facility. He presents the management perspective on the overall change, reporting lessons learned and results gained.

Bob Baxter is my name. I'm the general manager of production at Southcorp's Karadoc production facility. At the time of the introduction of self managing work teams into our operation, I was the packaging manager and hence my involvement in this process.

Southcorp Wines is Australia's largest producer of bottled and cask wine with annual sales in excess of $500 million dollars, a payroll of 2,400 people, and production facilities in three countries around the world. Wines from Australia are developing a good international reputation. However, Australian wineries compete with world wide wineries where much lower labour costs create a distinct disadvantage. Therefore, productivity is the key driver of business success. Australian wineries have adopted a variety of strategies to increase the international market share, including joint ventures. The key implication of their export focus is constant pressure to improve quality, reduce costs, and be flexible and responsive to marketing innovation requirements.

The Karadoc production facility is located in Victoria and is the largest of our Australian processing sites. It employs 300 people and produces an excess of 75 million litres of wine annually. Our business operation is focused on four organisational values:

♦ Providing outstanding value to our customers
♦ Delivering world class business performance
♦ Demonstrating that people are our most important resource
♦ Behaving with integrity

These four values are enshrined in our strategic plan, enterprise agreement, site department, and individual objectives. In pursuit of these values, we have continually challenged the management strategy, direction, and systems required to ensure progress and continuous improvement. Through this process of constant challenge, change and review, we have achieved significant improvement in areas of productivity, quality and safety performance.

Reasons for Changing

Despite this progress (and we were known throughout South-corp Wine as being very progressive in these areas) we realised that a number of deficiencies existed within our organisation that restricted our ability to successfully meet company objectives. It was this acknowledgement that led us down the path towards team development. The following were the major issues we faced at the time.

1. A requirement for a structure within our operation that facilitated effective decision making. Too many decisions were being made by supervisors without sufficient consultation with all interested parties. Often the resulting decision was less than adequate because all the relevant information was not being obtained and the appropriate people were not involved. Frequently there was insufficient commitment from operators to ensure the project's success, primarily because they had not been consulted.

2. We recognised that we were focusing on the control of people rather than the control of processes. We achieved this by directing all the actions and activities of our people. Any attempt by personnel to promote an alternative view was often seen as being disruptive. To challenge the status quo was not encouraged because managers knew better. (Isn't that why they were managers?)

3. There was an apparent lack of participation and commitment from a large section of our workforce. We did not actively encourage and seek out alternative views. We did encourage input that aligned with management thinking at the time, and often we promoted people because they supported the existing structure. The majority of our personnel were content to come to work, undertake the tasks required of them and go home at the end of the day with their pay. As long as we didn't challenge them, they wouldn't rock the boat.

4. We also found that our organisation was not sufficiently responsive to the needs of the modern day environment. The pace of change was increasing and we were struggling to manage that change. New product development, increasing quality standards, legislative requirements, and increased competition were testing our organisation. The complex chain of command with its rigid, formalised, and systematic approach to the management of these issues hindered our ability to deal effectively with them.

5. We realised that the existing structure was limiting the opportunities and development of our people. The traditional structure of operators, leading hands, supervisors, and managers provided little opportunity for advancement. But because the progression from operator to leading hand to supervisor was the only mechanism for promotion (or reward), we had continued the system.

6. Probably the most urgent reason for reviewing the structure of our operation was the increasing demands we were placing on our leading hands and supervisors. This key group were inundated with the sheer volume of work resulting from the various management programmes we had introduced since 1987 (in addition to controlling the workforce.)

There was clearly a need to introduce within our operation a structure that would address all of these deficiencies and develop a responsive, flexible, progressive, and challenging work environment.

Pilot Projects

At the time, (early 1990) a number of managers from our winery attended a conference on work redesign. This was our first introduction to team based operations and I can clearly remember my response to the presentation delivered by a general manager of a packaging enterprise based in Melbourne. 'The fellow's got rocks in his head,' would be a fairly appropriate translation. I have to admit, I was not impressed. 'Why would an organisation want to disrupt an operation in this manner in order to achieve improvement?' I said to myself. It was way beyond comprehension.

In late 1990, following exposure to other organisations' forays into the area of team development, and in response to a desire to improve the performance of one of our bottling lines, we commenced a trial with teams in our packaging operation. This pilot was undertaken on one of the smaller production lines at the time. In essence, the concept centred around removing the leading hand from the production line after consultation with those directly involved and working through the major issues when they surfaced.

This initial attempt to do self managing work teams failed for a number of reasons. We had not clearly identified what we were attempting to achieve. We didn't provide the resources like training to support the change. Few people in our organisation were committed to the concept. We didn't adequately sell to our employees the benefits of self managing teams. Many saw it as a management fad that would with time die a natural death and then allow them to get on with the job at hand.

We were motivated by the desire to reduce costs. The removal of a leading hand from the production line achieved a nominal 15% improvement in direct labour costs. From a production perspective that's pretty good. Unfortunately, this was more than offset by increased indirect costs, increased wastage, increased down time, confusion, and general disorder. The team was abandoned. The leading hand was returned to the line and everyone got back to work.

The next development occurred in 1993 and followed a review of the issues associated with our unsuccessful attempt to introduce team based structures into the organisation. Discussions resulted in the realisation that there were benefits to be gained by introducing self managing teams. (I must mention here that perseverance has to be one of the requirements to head down this path.) We decided to introduce another pilot team on one of our production lines.

For the bottling team, we first identified and selected four individuals who would be the team members. These people were chosen for their attitude to work and the organisation, their skills, and capabilities. A leading hand was selected to act as a co-ordinator for the team. Team goals were set and team values established. After four months, the team requested the co-ordinator be relocated. They believed they were more than capable of managing their team without the help of the co-ordinator. It appeared the co-ordinator was managing the team rather than providing a service. We removed the co-ordinator. After several months, we were quite encouraged by the success of this pilot, despite the fact that there were some issues. We agreed to develop self managing teams throughout the facility.

Total Workplace Redesign

The next stage involved the introduction of work teams right throughout the remainder of the packaging operation. We used participative design workshops to redesign the rest of the plant. The design workshops were crucial to the ongoing success and effectiveness of the new teams.

By this time the pilot line team had been in operation for almost twelve months. Many people within our organisation were questioning where we intended to progress next. Prior to introducing teams into the rest of the operation, we arranged meetings with all of our staff to explain the next steps and to ensure their involvement in the composition of the teams. The intention was to include everyone into the teams, and as such we did not have the luxury of picking and choosing selected operators as we had done previously.

At one of these meetings I was asked by one of our operators, 'What happens if we aren't successful? What happens if teams aren't a success? Do we go back to what we were doing before?' My response was that if we faced any difficulties, we'd identify the problems, plan a course of action to address those, and we would go forward with those modifications. The commitment of the organisation to team based operations was, as far as I was concerned, cast in stone. There was no return.

In participative design workshops, our operators established the team structures themselves, chose role personnel, and then commenced their training. The new structure has people on either bottling teams or packaging teams that are multi-skilled. Each team included role positions, such as quality, liaison, process improvement, rostering, and training. These teams have been in operation now for about three years. It has been probably the most challenging three years in our organisation's history. Throughout this period a number of issues have had to be addressed. They are:

Training for role people. These role people are now required to perform the functions previously required of the supervisors and leading hands, such as process improvement and quality. The training required has not always been adequate and on occasions has not been provided on a timely basis. In order for role people to undertake their responsibilities it is necessary for them to be relieved off the production line. The job requirements cannot be effectively followed through if this does not occur. For example, remedial action follow up, accident investigation, or reviewing the potential hazards associated with the introduction of new equipment requires time off line. If this is not provided then that follow up just does not happen. On occasions the role relief does not eventuate, e.g. someone is absent and the role relief person then is required to fill that line position.

143

Chapter 10
Making Wine
the Self
Managing Way
at Southcorp

Reluctance to participate. At times it is difficult to find volunteers to take on additional responsibilities (e.g. role positions) or to be team representatives on site committees. Some personnel are quite content to come to work and just do their job.

Maintaining focus on operational issues. At times the teams became distracted as a result of the development of interpersonal issues (on occasion the team meetings were referred to as 'bitch sessions.') Sometimes these interpersonal issues were not appropriately addressed (and at times management involvement and support was lacking) and therefore these issues consumed considerable time and energy.

Supervisors feeling out of control. A number of individuals (coincidentally many of these are from the supervisory level in the organisation) feel that there is not sufficient control of the people and processes. This is often due to their inability to accept change, but also due to the fact that at times the control of processes has not always been adequate. This was due to a lack of understanding of requirements, deficiencies in training, lack of support, and poorly established goals and targets.

One of the greatest difficulties we faced was the management of the supervisors and leading hands. This group of people had the most to lose as a result of the change. A number of supervisors displayed excellent technical skills and that technical expertise was still required by our teams. Our greatest challenge was to integrate the supervisors into the new structure. Some who had specialist skills were utilised to provide support. This support took the form of role training, lesson plan development, relief of team members and role personnel in order to allow project work to be undertaken, and assistance in the area of problem solving and troubleshooting. Others, following counselling sessions, were incorporated into the teams as team members. It sometimes took quite a few sessions to resolve that issue. We had a couple of our leading hands who were quite happy to go back into line positions. The greatest difficulty in what we did in this whole process of team development was to prevent the supervisors and leading hands from reverting to their previous management style.

145

Chapter 10
Making Wine
the Self
Managing Way
at Southcorp

Performance Measures

We haven't removed all controls. We manage the business by measuring agreed outcomes rather than by controlling the details associated with how those outcomes are to be achieved. This allows our employees the freedom to determine the most appropriate methodology or means for achieving those outcomes themselves.

A comprehensive series of performance measures have been developed for the whole organisation relating to site, department, team, and individual objectives. In all there are about 50 performance measures covering the site. These measures are based around the four organisation values.

The measures are collated monthly and the results are reported to everyone. We have a performance payment scheme that is related to our achievement against these indicators. This system relies on all seven departments on site achieving their objectives prior to their payment being met. It is a site payment that we make. If one department falls down, the whole site is affected by that performance. What we've seen as a result of that is a tendency for other departments to come to the assistance of a particular department that may be having some trouble meeting its objectives. Not only that, we also find that often to achieve a particular objective three or four departments need to work together.

We also measure the impact of change on our people. On a performance quarterly basis we undertake a survey to measure the impact of change on our organisation and its people. Following the survey process, each department selects a particular area that requires improvement, determines action plans, and endeavours to improve their rating in that particular area. What we are measuring here is whether or not people are more satisfied in these particular areas (the six criteria for productive work) than they were previously; whether there is no change in their satisfaction level; or whether they are less satisfied.

This process of involvement of our people in business performance measurement has assisted in achieving increased accountability with our staff. Some of our people have welcomed the freedom allowed them in this process of contributing and involvement in the decision making process. Others have found it very challenging. Everyone has to participate and contribute, each according to his or her abilities. This is a message we are constantly reviewing with all our people. It has also required a change in focus by our managers. Each manager is required to champion one of the site's management programmes and drive that process through the organisation.

Our organisation, as it's progressed down the path of self management, has required our managers to change their contribution to the new organisation's structure. No longer do our managers have the ability to direct what shall be done. They must be prepared to be challenged when they do infringe in areas of responsibility that are no longer within their jurisdiction. Many of our managers have taken umbrage when this has occurred. In our organisation, the requirements that we demand from our managers have changed quite radically. Their role is to establish through consultation the measures of performance for the business and then provide the resources to those people who are managing the process, to enable them to achieve the mutually agreed outcomes. They have a responsibility in the management of boundaries – those issues that cross functional areas or departments and those issues developing from outside the organisation which influence and affect business performance.

They also provide personal development to their staff, that is, provide them with the skills which will enable them to manage the challenges facing the organisation. The greatest failing of most of our managers involved in this area is their inability to keep out of team business. All too often, managers will step in and make decisions for the teams or commit the teams to courses of action that, while it might have been in the best interest of the business, was certainly not in the best interest of the team.

Often, because clearly defined outcomes were not established, it became necessary for our managers to become involved in order to keep the business on track. On the other hand, it is important for the managers to provide support and become involved when requested. I have seen several instances in our organisation when a manager who has been asked for help has responded, 'That's a team issue, you resolve it!' In a number of these instances the team has not been capable of dealing with that issue and has needed the manager's input. The challenge for our managers is to find the right balance.

I'd like here to recount a couple of comments made recently by a member of the management team. This was a discussion about the introduction of the self managing work teams.

> 'It was like we were on a train and you (Bob) were in the engine and we were back in the caboose. It was frustrating for the staff because there was Bob heading off with a vision that we hadn't had time to effectively digest. You'd had several months to come to terms with what was happening, but to us it was all new. We also believed that teams were just for the production people. It was OK for them to be in teams but we managers – were different.'

I asked her what it was that convinced the management team and the administration people to come on board and actively support the direction we were taking. She said:

> 'At one of our meetings several months after the introduction of the teams into the production area, when you asked what would happen if people didn't support the direction, the response you gave to us made us realise that you were serious. To be told that people who don't fit into the new culture will fall by the wayside made us realise that we had better come on board.'

147

Chapter 10
Making Wine
the Self
Managing Way
at Southcorp

She continued,

'I recall the day that you discussed with all of the packaging people following the Bottling team pilot and prior to introducing teams into the rest of the operation. When we saw the expression on the packaging operators' faces and realised that most of them were terrified about what was about to occur, we realised that we (management that is) weren't under any threat at all and that the operators would need our assistance. The office personnel weren't 100% supportive but realised that they would all sink or swim together and that they certainly weren't going to sink.'

Critical Success Factors

A mature culture that readily accepts change is essential for the successful implementation of self managing work teams. Without this, the challenges confronting those involved will prove too great and the process will falter. We've seen evidence of this in other divisions of our organisation within Australia.

It is also important to identify the benefits of the change process for all stakeholders and clearly communicate those benefits. If we are unable to convey benefits to our people, we shouldn't be surprised if they don't wish to become involved and are less than committed.

Without commitment, the exercise will fail. The process does need to be driven and will only succeed if it is driven from the very top. The commitment required must also be visible. There needs to be tangible evidence that this is not just another management fad and the exercise is being implemented just to increase productivity. Management will need to show evidence that it will live by the new rules. Actions speak louder than words.

One of the most tangible means of displaying commitment is by the provision of the resources required to facilitate the change process. We view the resources required as an investment. Investments frequently have little or no short term benefits. Training is by far the greatest commitment required. It would be appropriate to acknowledge that we didn't provide as much training as we could have. We would have been more successful if we had provided a better overview of what we were doing and why and followed this up with more intensive specific team training. We should have also provided more general management training to the teams in areas such as planning, organising, problem solving, and communication.

One of the greatest challenges that we faced is the management of interpersonal issues associated with self managing work teams. In a traditional structure, the leading hand or supervisor would manage those issues that arbitrate between individuals, enforce discipline, and maintain standards of performance. While employees didn't often approve of the decisions being made by the supervisors, they did accept that the supervisors had the authority to make them. It was also convenient for them to have someone to blame. When the supervisors were removed and the team itself is faced with the challenge of managing these interpersonal issues, considerable conflict does result.

I would estimate that probably at present we have 30-40% of our people who are totally committed to what we are doing and very enthusiastic about it. Fifty to sixty percent are reasonably comfortable with what we are doing and participate and we have about 10% who, as I have said here, are uncomfortable with the concept; it would probably be more accurate to say that, wherever they get an opportunity, they are attempting to work against it. With time, we will effectively deal with those people. Our objective is to assure that the 50-60% that are sort of sitting on the fence become very committed; the 10% that aren't will leave. Before we do that we'll address their concerns and issues. We will counsel them and we'll discuss with them how we can go about addressing those issues. But the commitment to what we are doing is final and ultimately it will be their choice. A number of people have left our organisation over the past three or four years because they have found that they are uncomfortable with where we are headed.

149

Chapter 10
Making Wine
the Self
Managing Way
at Southcorp

Benefits of Team based Design

Over the past two years we have clearly identified the benefits associated with the process of empowerment.

People
In
Charge

1. As a result of greater worker involvement in the management of our operation, there has been an improvement in the organisation's responsiveness to change. Several years ago, when introducing new products or packaging redesigns, we seldom met our time frames and often experienced difficulties. Currently we are achieving a 100% success rate with the introduction of new packaging and all recent projects have been launched ahead of schedule.

2. This process has assisted in the further development of a mature and responsible organisational culture. The benefits that this brings to an operation is many fold and includes harmonious industrial relations, a positive attitude to the company, a more committed workforce and a greater acceptance of and commitment towards change.

3. Through this process we are actively promoting and developing people with a sense of social responsibility. The benefit that the organisation achieves here is the development of personnel as ambassadors for the organisation.

4. Commitment to improvement activities. Through the development of team goals we are ensuring that our people are more focused on the critical business outcomes and results. Associated with this is their involvement in the activities that will result in improvements in productivity, waste reduction, quality improvements, and service levels. Because our people have the intimate understanding and knowledge of the process, their involvement is crucial to the process of improvement and the success of any change implemented.

5. Cost reductions. The results achieved with our pilot programmes demonstrated that productivity improvements will be

achieved. We are currently achieving annual efficiency savings of approximately 7%.

6. Material wastage levels have reduced from over 3.2% to less than 0.4%. Wine losses have been reduced by 60% in the last two years.

7. Quality. Team based structures with their greater sense of ownership have resulted in significant gains in the area of quality improvements. Standards of quality are now much higher and the levels of rejects are now lower than we have ever seen. Initially the levels of rejected product rose as our people demonstrated their commitment to dispatching only that product that met agreed standards and specification.

8. Safety performance. The site's lost time injury frequency rate has declined from just under 20 to zero in the last six years.

9. Trust. We are finding that our people are developing greater trust in the organisation as a consequence of being treated in a consistent, responsible and mature manner. As a consequence of being involved in the decision making process they also have a greater understanding of the challenges facing organisations and the difficulties associated with making decisions that are acceptable to all stakeholders. We share the organisation's financial performance information with our workforce. Our rationale here is that if the organisation is profitable this provides greater security of employment and improves our opportunities for growth, (in the last ten years our site has doubled its throughput.)

Self managing teams are a means towards the end. They are a tool in the process of continuous improvement that will result in the development of the potential of all the employees in our organisation. There is not one structure that is correct or right for an organisation. There are a number of factors that will have to be taken into account during the evolution process. The culture of the business will play an important role in this process of evolution as will the nature of the business and the existing

151

Chapter 10
Making Wine
the Self
Managing Way
at Southcorp

structure. What is important is the understanding of the principles involved in the concept, and, more importantly, the motivation for the introduction of self managing teams. For if the right concept is introduced for the wrong reason, it will quickly flounder. At Karadoc we believe it is important to be innovative in the way we manage our people. Innovation in the area of people management and development will provide the competitive edge, we believe, that will be difficult to match. It is through team development that we will achieve this competitive edge.

Bob Baxter of Southcorp Wines presented this case at the Fifth European Ecology of Work Conference in Dublin, Ireland in May 1997.

E-mail: bob.d.baxter@southcorp.com.au

Bob Baxter worked with Amerin's **Peter Aughton** *and* **Sam Joukadjian** *on self management at Southcorp Wines.*

Email: melboffice@amerin.com.au

Chapter 11

Team Based Management In The U.S. Courts

by David K. Hendrickson

How can a small government agency in Washington, D.C. help bring team based management to the widely dispersed, highly decentralised, and traditionally hierarchical federal court system? This was a dilemma faced by the Federal Judicial Center in 1993. This chapter is the story of how we developed a nation wide support system to introduce and nurture the team based approach in the federal system of district courts, bankruptcy courts, probation offices, and pre-trial services offices in 96 districts, each with its own independent management hierarchy.

The Federal Judicial Center is a tiny (by U.S. Government standards) independent agency charged with supporting the courts through training and research. It has no authority to coerce any of the nearly 400 federal court units to do anything, let alone try a totally new management approach. Its only avenue for change is to provide an attractive service and hope that someone will take advantage of it.

The story of how we built a successful support system for teams may interest other organisations that want to introduce team based management into a widely dispersed and decentralised system, whether in government or in the private sector. This is the story of how we initially sought assistance from outside to develop a framework for change, then developed a system for introducing and supporting change from within. Internal support was fostered by building a network of peer consultants. These peer facilitators helped court managers with training and consultation throughout their court's transition to self managing teams.

This big idea began with a limited idea and grew into something we never imagined. In the beginning, we were looking for ways we could help courts become more efficient through training. We often convene planning groups made up of managers from our client courts to explore their training needs and plan the development of future programs. In 1993 we convened such a group. We were faced with a motivating challenge. The federal court system, up until that time, had largely avoided the pressures to do more with less that was already being felt in private industry and some other areas of government. For the first time, the courts were coming under fire. Budgets were being reduced. Rather than throwing new money and new staff at problems, management was now being asked to be a little more creative in their use of scarce resources. The purpose of our meeting was helping the courts do their work more effectively and efficiently with fewer resources.

We asked Bob Rehm, a consultant with broad experience in organisation development, to help us facilitate the meeting. We invited court managers who we knew were in the vanguard of progressive thinking about management. Some of them were already using some form of teams or elements of total quality in their own courts, at a time when this was not the norm in the federal court system. The discussion was intense, and lasted for three days. The crucial point came when the group asked if they could go beyond the original scope of their mission: 'A mere day long training program or two will not address the issues we need to deal with – we need long term consultation and support for major organisational change.' We agreed to support this venture in its newly enlarged scope.

We hammered out an ambitious plan. The basis of it was the Center would support three initiatives for change in the courts. Helping individual courts move into using self managing teams was one of the three. The other two were total quality management and process improvement. For each of the three, the Center would develop a range of support resources, including handbooks, workshops, inter-court visits, and a network of peer consultants. In addition to these direct resources, the Center would publicise the project and provide information about it to interested court units. Since participation in the project was voluntary, marketing the changes would be crucial to its success.

One of our goals was to create a system of support for teams that would be native to the federal court system. We wanted to build up expertise amongst court managers who could then help each other, rather than relying on the assistance of outside consultants. Consultants would be important in helping us design and build this system, but at some point it should become self sustaining.

155

Chapter 11
Team Based
Management
In The
U.S. Courts

The first step in building this system of support was to train a corps of court managers in how to conduct the team workshop. Bob Rehm agreed to conduct a training for facilitators program. We invited thirteen court managers from around the country to attend. We wanted this group to inspire confidence among their peers, other top court managers who would be requesting the workshop for the staff in their districts. To inspire the confidence of their peers, we chose people based on the following criteria. First, they should be either a top administrator in a court unit (clerk of court, chief probation officer, etc.), or a close affiliate also in the top management team. Second, they should have experience in using teams in their own districts. Third, and harder to quantify, they should have a passionate interest and belief in the system of values underlying the team concept.

At the training for facilitators workshop, we learned about the participative design workshop and the design principles underlying it. We learned how to conduct the various activities that are keystones of the workshop, and the facilitators practised conducting the workshop on each other. But there was an important element of a real workshop that was difficult to simulate in a training setting: the social dynamics of a real group of co-workers charged with redesigning their organisation into teams. We tried to make up for this as best we could, talking about different situations and problems that could arise during a real workshop, and how to deal with them productively to move the group ahead into team formation.

Despite the preparation at the training for facilitators workshop, everyone felt that doing the first real workshop in the courts would be an adventure. We weren't sure we were ready for all it could throw our way. We were very nervous about the prospect of going into a district at management's request, stirring up a lot of expectations with talk about teams, and then leaving. There was a good bit of worry about 'going in and messing up someone else's district.' Therefore we tried to plan as many ways as we could to prepare the client districts and ourselves so there wouldn't be any unmanageable surprises.

To help assuage the facilitators' fears about the unknown dynamics they might encounter, we decided to send Bob and me along to back them up the first time they conducted a workshop. This proved to be a very sound step, since it helped us out in several ways. First, it built up the facilitators' confidence and gave them the courage to do whatever was needed to keep a workshop on track, including making audacious decisions if there was a clear need for them. It helped also for Bob and me to see each facilitator at work and give individualised guidance to help develop their skills.

The wisdom of providing experienced back-up was proved the first time we conducted the workshop, in the District Court in Sacramento, California. The facilitators had conducted a series of conference calls with the court's management beforehand, to discuss what design issues were and were not on the table, how the space should be set up, and who should attend the workshop. During this consultation phase, we made a mistake which came back to haunt us during the workshop itself. The court's management felt strongly that they would like to include the courtroom deputies in the design workshop, even though their own work would not be up for redesign. It seemed an innocent enough request, and we assented. But when we got into the design phase of the workshop itself, it became apparent that this had been a big mistake. The court staff whose work was being redesigned consisted of docket clerks, file clerks, and intake clerks. They were already uncertain about the intent of this workshop which was claiming to let them decide how they organised their work. The courtroom deputies, safely shielded from any change to their own work, set about giving the other clerks their ideas about how they should change the way they did things. The clerks could not get down to redesigning their work as long as they felt someone else was trying to tell them how to do it. There was gridlock in the workshop.

'What can we do?' we asked ourselves, somewhat at a loss how to proceed. We quickly decided that we had to get the courtroom deputies out of the workshop. This was something that I, as an experienced curriculum developer, had never done before: asking a good number of the participants to leave halfway through the program. It was an alarming prospect, but not so alarming as letting the workshop fail. So after our break, the facilitators announced that we had come to a transitional point in the workshop, and we were moving from the inform-ational portion to the redesign portion. At this point, we wanted to thank the courtroom deputies for sharing their input into the process, and excuse them from the rest of the workshop. This occasioned some consternation and spirited discussion, but in the end was successful, in no small part due to the conciliatory words of one of the courtroom deputies. She said that she could well understand the need for the participants to work together privately at this stage, and wished them well.

After that, things turned around in the workshop. Without the non-participants, the group that was left was able to focus on redesigning their own work. There were some more bumps and glitches along the way, but in the end they put together a satisfactory design that launched them into their new teams successfully. Over the years, the original design evolved to meet the changing needs of the teams, but we also learned that this was to be expected.

As we began to implement the workshop in more districts, we learned more lessons about how to make the workshop successful, and how to foster the growth of teams in the courts. One lesson was the importance of preparing the court for change. Before we go to a court to conduct a workshop, there is a sequence of steps that we now go through to help them prepare. The first is a series of discussions with management about what the change to teams means, and how it will change the dynamics of the office and the way they manage. This is done by conference calls with the facilitators. We usually include not only the top level of management in the target court, but intermediate management, and often supervisors as well. We discuss any constraints that limit the potential scope of the redesign, so that it can be clear from the start what is on the table and what is not. We may suggest articles to read for management and staff to give a sense of what team based management entails.

To help orient the target court to the potential changes of team based management, we developed a half hour videotape showing staff in team courts doing their work, holding team meetings, 'huddling' to allot work or solve a problem as it arises. The videotape also gives a preview of what to expect in the team workshop. This portion of the tape was shot during an actual workshop in one of the courts that was making the transition to teams. It shows design groups working on various tasks, and the whole group presenting their final design to the clerk of court. Finally, actual court employees talked about how teams had changed their work for the better. We found that a tape portraying peers from within the federal court system was much more effective at gaining the interest and acceptance of court managers and staff than a generic or commercial videotape would have been, because it made a much stronger connection to work they were familiar with.

Likewise, it has been extraordinarily helpful to be able to rely on experienced court managers as workshop facilitators and consultants to the interested courts. Since they speak the language of the courts, these facilitators make an immediate connection with their peers. Since they also have experience with teams in their own courts, they can talk knowledgeably about different team configurations that make sense in a court context, and can offer advice on how to be supportive of the teams without taking over their work. While there is no technical reason that the facilitators conducting a team workshop should require specific knowledge about the type of organisation which is changing to teams, coming from a similar background has a psychological advantage in that it lends the facilitators greater credibility in the participants' eyes.

Familiarity with the court environment presents a danger as well as an advantage. The danger is that the workshop facilitators will fall into the role of 'experts' and the workshop participants will depend on them for answers rather than working together to come up with a solution that makes sense for them. In the beginning, it is especially tempting for facilitators to slip into the expert role when they see work groups struggling with design tasks that the facilitators have already dealt with in their own districts. I have been to several of our early workshops where this started to happen. Participants, who are often daunted by the tasks they have to struggle with, may latch onto the expertise of the facilitators as a way out. Once this pattern of reliance rather than independence is established, it can be hard to get the work groups to do their own work. It seems so much easier to find out how someone else has configured their teams, rather than struggling with what makes sense in your own situation.

161

Chapter 11
Team Based
Management
In The
U.S. Courts

This is another situation where having expert guidance of experienced consultants early on was a help to us. Whenever a pattern of dependence on the facilitators began to emerge in an early workshop, one of the experienced consultants would approach the facilitators during an off time, and point out what was going on, encouraging them to pull back and return the work to the participants. Facilitators were encouraged to leave the groups from time to time rather than being constantly available to help them. Or they might reply to requests for assistance with answers like 'You are the experts in how things are done here, and you know a lot more about it than I do – that's something you will have to figure out for yourselves.' With a little coaching and practice, all of our facilitators mastered this technique.

There is a delicate balance that the facilitators must walk between giving too much help and too little. There is little point in letting an entire workshop bog down while a group struggles down a road that the facilitator knows is an unfruitful one. This is part of the 'art' of conducting the team workshop. It requires judgement calls. A guiding principle that is useful is for the facilitators to ask themselves which course of action is most likely to enable the work groups to continue productively in their work of becoming more like self managing teams.

In addition to establishing a support system for courts interested in moving to teams, we had to develop a system for attracting their attention in the first place and making them want to try out the team approach. Since the Federal Judicial Center, as I mentioned, is a government agency whose mission is to support the highly independent network of court units throughout the country, each of which has its own management, we had to market the team approach to these, our clients. Unlike some large corporations or other organisations, we could not mandate change, we could only present information about how to change, and provide assistance to anyone who was interested.

The cornerstone of our marketing strategy was a series of three day orientation programs for top court managers. At these orientations, they could learn from their peers about how they were using the three targeted management strategies: teams, total quality management, and process improvement. The 'carrot' to this approach was the opportunity to travel to Washington, D.C. to attend an orientation at Center expense, to gain exposure to new ideas, and to network with peers. This 'carrot' was accompanied by a subtle 'stick' – the implicit change in the way the federal government and the courts were operating. The pressure to 'do more with less' which had been felt for some time in the private sector, was overtaking the government. Budgets were being tightened, often in areas previously shielded from the paring knives of budget cutters. At the same time, more autonomy was being allowed for local units to try innovative solutions, so there was the opportunity, as well as the pressure, for positive change.

Most of the time at the orientation programs was devoted to panels of court managers with experience in using one of the three strategies in their own districts. In the case of teams, we included supervisors and team members on the panel to give a full perspective. It was interesting that the team panel was always the one that created the most controversy. Courts are traditionally fairly conservative organisations and tend to have a hierarchical heritage. Reactions therefore were highly mixed. Audiences asked lots of hard questions and panels were direct and honest in their replies, telling about the difficulties that they had run into as well as the advantages they had reaped. One group of managers was immediately attracted to the team approach, and many of them said that it was exactly what they had been looking for, but didn't quite know how to implement on their own. Others were interested, but not ready to take action until they saw how things worked out for the pioneers. A small but vocal third group was appalled by what they perceived as the team approach's challenge to traditional authority. I will never forget one particular orientation where the overall program received one of the best and one of the absolute worst written evaluations of any program that I have ever presented, including one accusing the Center of advocating communism! We also sent panels to speak at annual conferences of court managers, and published articles and announcements about the three strategies in the court managers' professional publications. All of these efforts paid off in time, as more and more court units adopted one or more of the strategies and saw significant positive results from it. To date, twenty three court units have used the teams workshop to redesign themselves into a democratic, self managing organisational style. Another sixteen have moved into teams on their own, without using the workshop to get started.

As more and more courts began implementing team structures, we sought ways to provide support to them beyond the initial consultation and start up workshop. Both managers and team members expressed their desire to learn more about what their peers were doing in other districts. To accommodate this desire, we set up a series of two on-line conferences in which court staff could engage in an ongoing dialogue about team issues via their computers and the Internet. We created these conferences using Caucus software, which allowed us to create an asynchronous learning environment. By asynchronous, what is meant is that, unlike a live chat room or a live training session, everyone does not have to be present at once. Participants log on whenever it is convenient for them to do so, read messages from other participants, and respond if they wish with their own thoughts and contributions. The conference is a running transcript of an ongoing exchange of messages. To create some structure in this format, a conference organiser sets up 'discussion items,' equivalent to topics or concurrent sessions at a live conference. Participants who want to discuss pay structures as they relate to teams, or the changing roles of former supervisors, can visit items set up on those topics. These on-line conferences provided an inexpensive avenue for thoughtful dialogue among participants all around the country, without the necessity to leave their work places to travel to a workshop in a distant city. We found them to be a fruitful forum for the exchange of ideas.

Another form of support for team courts which we made use of was the traditional live workshop. On two occasions, we sponsored live national workshops in which participants from around the country travelled to a central location for three days of sharing and learning with their peers. We created an interesting and highly successful format for these workshops.

Half of each workshop consisted of traditional training sessions on team related topics led by expert consultants. The other half consisted of 'open space' sessions where participants met for informal discussions with others who shared a passionate interest or concern around the same topic. The open space format fits beautifully with the concept of self managing teams, because it gives conference participants control over setting the agenda, creating the sessions, and deciding what sessions they want to attend. While it might seem that such an approach would be chaotic, there is enough structure in the open space design to make it work, if the group has a high proportion of dedicated individuals with a passionate interest in the topic. (For more information about open space, see Harrison Owen's book, *Open Space Technology.*)

One benefit of both the on-line and live national workshops is that they allowed team members to network with their peers from other courts. Often in the courts, as in most large, widely dispersed organisations, it is the upper and middle levels of management that profit from a disproportionate percentage of formal training. By allowing line level staff members from teams to participate in our conferences, we afforded a valuable opportunity to learn, share, and network to many individuals who had never participated before in a national training program.

The change to teams has enabled courts to achieve several different goals. The goal that perhaps speaks loudest to Congress is financial. By making better use of staffing resources, several team courts have been able to complete a high volume of quality work at reduced staffing levels. They have been able to use the extra funds to purchase needed equipment or otherwise improve operations and services. At least one court has returned nearly a million dollars from its budget to the central government in a gain sharing agreement, which also allowed them to distribute part of the gain to staff in the form of bonuses for the extra work done per staff member.

But the most palpable change to the people involved in the change to teams has been the change in the quality of their work life. Individual team members interviewed for our videotape[1] on team based management say it best:

> 'People are much happier being in the role of decision making for their own destiny. They're in the best position to make some positive changes.'

> 'We have people who are enthusiastic about their work, who are spontaneous, and who give one hundred and ten percent.'

> 'Everybody feels like they have more say and they know more about what's going on in the office.'

'It's completely different than working with a work leader or supervisors. It cuts out the chain of command, and makes you the chain. You are the chain of command.'

'This is the first place I've ever worked where everybody acts like adults and does a very good job.'

'It's consistent with how I feel people ought to be treated, where I think the know how is and where I think the authority and responsibility lie.'

There are a large number of people around the country now benefiting from this program.[2] We have every possible type of court unit implementing team based management – pre-trial services, probation, bankruptcy and district courts, including some of the smallest and some of the largest units in the country.

David Hendrickson *is a Curriculum Development Specialist for the Federal Judicial Center in Washington, D.C.*
David develops training programs and other forms of support for the U.S. Courts.

E-mail: dhendric@fjc.gov

Chapter 12

Western Washington Clerk's Office: Our Journey Into Self Managing Teams

Janet Bubnis

Janet Bubnis tells the remarkable story of her organisation's transformation into a self managing workplace. Reading it reminded me of a great moment in my work redesign experience. The scene was the final day in the redesign of the Seattle district court office that is the subject of this chapter. The new self managing teams were presenting their action plans to one another. Bruce Rifkin, Clerk of Court, was in the room listening intently. Several of the teams reported the need for an additional member because of their concerns about team workloads. They thought Bruce should hire someone new for their team. As the last team finished its presentation, you could feel the tension in the room. Everyone was awaiting Bruce's reaction. Bruce took a deep breath and said this to the new teams: 'Welcome to the world of management!' People gazed in disbelief as it began to sink in that this change was 'for real.' Bruce continued, 'I see some good planning here. But regarding your desires for additional staff, let me say this. We have one position budgeted, and several requests. Now that we are a self managing workplace, let the negotiations begin among us. We're all in charge now.' Over the next few weeks Bruce and the teams sorted out their staffing needs. The change to self management was under way. Here's the story.

I am the chief deputy clerk in a mid-size U.S. District Court Clerk's Office in the Pacific Northwest. Clerk of Court Bruce Rifkin and I were among those court managers who David Hendrickson of the Federal Judicial Center (FJC) brought back to Washington, DC in 1994, to be trained as facilitators for the participative design workshop. We had been interested in teams for some time, but weren't sure how to go about implementing them. We had long been proponents of a decentralised and participatory management style, but were puzzled why our staff didn't seem to feel or act empowered. We hoped that this new FJC program would give us better insights into how to turn our ideas into reality.

Learning how to facilitate the various workshop activities was easy enough, and we were curious about how it would work in a real court setting. Bruce and I were the facilitators who Bob Rehm and David Hendrickson coached in the first judiciary workshop in Sacramento, California. The experience astonished us! The descriptions you've read throughout this book about the participative design workshop give you a good understanding of its activities, and it's easy to see how they lead participants into the redesign process. What an objective, reasoned description fails to communicate, however, is the almost frightening level of energy that it unleashes! As a novice facilitator I felt ill equipped to channel all of that intensity; today, with a bit more experience under my belt, I'm no longer frightened by it, but instead find it extremely challenging and exhilarating. It was clear to Bruce and me that this was the catalyst we'd been looking for.

Upon returning to our own court, we made plans to conduct the workshop within the next several months. We decided that all parts of our office would make the transition into self managing teams as part of a week-long series of workshops. The staff had previously been organised into functional units (docketing, intake, automation, etc.), and it made sense to them to retain these functional relationships within a team. These units had supervisors, who participated in the workshop with the staff they used to supervise, and they used the workshop as a first step in exploring what their new roles would be. In some instances the supervisors were absorbed into the teams, with no more authority than any other team member. In other instances, the teams did not feel that the supervisors belonged within the teams, so these ex-supervisors were left to figure out among themselves what their new roles would be. In all instances, staff walked into the workshop as members of a supervised unit, and walked out as members of a self managing team.

The Early Months

I'm not sure any of us really understood what lay ahead when we started in 1994. Self management was new for the staff, and required of them skills they weren't confident they possessed. Learning to deal with teams rather than individuals, and to bite our tongues when we wanted to give solutions rather than reassurance, were difficult adjustments for us managers. And the poor ex-supervisors were left with great anxiety about their status and value within this new organisation. Not surprisingly, there were some bumpy periods. Perhaps it could have gone smoother had we implemented teams more gradually, but in hindsight we're convinced that these growing pains were necessary elements in changing the culture of the office and building cohesive teams.

Early issues within the teams

From the very beginning, our teams accepted full responsibility for their work. Many began providing services in a way that was more holistic and focused on the overall court, rather than being focused on individual jobs or 'their' judges. Despite struggling with interpersonal and inter-team issues, the quality, timeliness, and customer service aspects of their work products were never in serious question.

Every one of our teams decided to embrace the full range of supervisory responsibilities immediately, and were very sensitive to any hint of outside interference or internal bossiness. Certainly they tested us to see if we really would let them make their own decisions, including bad ones. If anyone outside the team was critical of one of them, they 'circled the wagons' and defended their member regardless of the accuracy of the criticism. They were loath to ask for help even when they were floundering because they interpreted that as a sign that they had failed in self management. They tended to hire people they felt comfortable with, people who didn't intimidate them. And not surprisingly, they were very reticent about giving each other candid feedback about performance and conduct.

None of these issues is very surprising. In fact, we believe they may be natural steps in the evolution of mature teams. Facing the consequences of their own poor choices or inaction is far more effective than all the nagging in the world! Mutual trust, or the lack thereof, was a big problem in many of the teams – for these groups we provided the opportunity to meet with professional counsellors to help them grow as a team. For other teams the problem was one of denial and refusal to acknowledge serious personnel issues – for them, having the problem escalate until it became a crisis was a powerful lesson in the futility of trying to maintain a pretense of wellness.

Early issues with the former supervisors

The poor middle managers! Bruce, Janet Thornton (the deputy-in-charge in the field office), and I still kept our roles as management, and the teams were empowered with new authority, but what were the former supervisors supposed to do? Unfortunately, we were able to offer little concrete guidance. We had heard that other organisations used their former supervisors as trainers, quality control experts, and coaches. But our newly formed teams wanted to develop their own internal capacity for training and quality control, and at least initially they were suspicious of outside coaches, particularly in the form of ex-supervisors. Those supervisors who were absorbed within their teams seemed to have an easier go of it at first, although many of these arrangements deteriorated over time. The supervisors who were cut loose from the teams came to work the following week with no clear sense of what they were supposed to do. Bruce insisted that their new roles had to flow out of what the office and the teams needed from them, and since it took time for us and them to figure that out, the ex-supervisors went through some very difficult times. It's easy to see why at times they developed resentment towards the teams that had 'rejected' them and were now making mistakes that never would have happened if the supervisors had remained in place.

This too was probably necessary in the teams' and the ex-supervisors' growth. Had the supervisors remained absorbed within the teams, or had they retained roles as primary coaches and trainers for the staff they used to supervise – in short, functioned as a safety net – the teams might not have reached their full potential. And the ex-supervisors certainly wouldn't have found their new role as an empowered and integrated 'middle.' (More about that later).

Early issues with management

For Bruce, Janet, and me, the hardest part was developing a sense of timing and proportion in our dealings with teams. Too much intervention, or too soon, resulted in our assuming 'ownership' of the problem; too little or too late, and the team floundered and lost confidence in its abilities. We tended to notice issues developing earlier than the teams were comfortable with acknowledging them. If we pressed too hard, they simply disowned it as their problem. We therefore found it necessary to bite our tongues and let the issue 'ripen.' Letting them make mistakes and face the consequences for them was probably the most difficult thing we had to do.

One incident in particular stands out. One team was recruiting to fill a vacancy, and at the end of the interviewing process came to us with a recommendation for hiring. In reviewing the applicant's resumé it was obvious that this young man had far fewer skills and less experience than most staff we hire. I questioned the team about this, and they defended their choice because they said his interpersonal skills were excellent and they thought he would fit in well. I was aware that the person who previously held this position had been very bright, abrasive, and abrupt, and feared that the team was placing too much importance upon this applicant's comfortable personality. I asked them to go back through the resumés of applicants, select another five or six based solely on merit, interview them, then come back to me with their recommendation. The team did as I asked, but after that additional day of interviewing they reconfirmed that they still wanted their original choice. Bruce and I assented.

Before the first six months was up this young man had demonstrated a pattern of work-related errors, lack of professionalism in his demeanour and dealings with others, and on one occasion failed to come to work because he had been over-celebrating the night before. This last infraction earned him a formal reprimand. Both he and the team took stock of the situation. They told him that they went out on a limb for him and now their credibility was on the line. They emphasised their commitment to his success and proposed to appoint one of them as his mentor. He, in turn, was overwhelmed by this support and concern from the team. He came to Bruce and said that he had 'blown off' jobs in the past, but could not do that with this job because these were good people who believed in him and who didn't deserve to have him let them down. He recommitted himself to succeeding on the job. The long and the short of it is that this was clearly a poor hiring decision; we let the team make that decision; and they faced the consequences when he faltered and embarrassed all of them.

The end of this story is yet to be written, however. He remains part of our staff today, still a little rough around the edges, but a strong advocate of teams both inside and outside our office. He's one of the most effective speakers I take with me when we make presentations to other Clerk's Offices because staff can relate to his story and to how his team helped him through his rocky start. Today, he's smart on the computer, helpful and supportive of his team-mates, and adds a certain humour, enthusiasm, and leadership to that group that make him a definite asset. And as a final note, the two new staff that this team has hired since then have been persons of maturity, solid experience, and excellent skills.

Today, self managing teams seem so natural that we don't even think of them as anything special any longer. Over the years, our teams have routinely taken responsibility for hiring new employees, coordinating their training, giving feedback to each other, conducting formal performance appraisals, recommending pay increases, documenting performance and recommending disciplinary actions when necessary, distributing work and arranging coverage for absences, and experimenting with new ideas for improving the workplace. They have taken an active role in searching out the training they need to equip themselves for handling this range of activities.

The problems we have now in 1999 are not that different from the normal problems you would always expect to have in any organisation – the difficulty of dealing with individual performance and conduct problems, adapting to new technologies and processes, and keeping up with increasing workload in the face of diminishing resources. Our teams have, by and large, developed good internal cohesion. Good communication and collaboration between teams remain a challenge.

Every so often, when we have a group of 5-6 new employees, I call them together for a mini-teams session, to explain to them where we came from, what 'teams' mean in our environment, and where I think we're going. I ask for their comments regarding their early experiences in their different teams and how this compares with other jobs they've held. All speak of the initial shock of being interviewed by a whole roomful of people (most teams have as many of their members as possible participate). But then they report the great feeling of coming to work on that first day knowing that your co-workers have chosen you and are committed to your success. They also voice appreciation for how willing everyone is to share information, as opposed to the information hoarding they experienced in other jobs, and the incredible supportiveness and helpfulness of their team-mates. They're excited about the encouragement they receive for personal growth and skill-enhancement, even in areas not directly related to the job. They feel an atmosphere

Chapter 12
Western
Washington
Clerk's Office

that they haven't felt in other jobs. After they've been here for a year or more, most would never want to go back to any other way of working.

What About the 'Odds and Ends'?

Start-up and growing pains

When we converted to teams, we had a number of staff who didn't fit easily into a functional group with others. These included a budget officer, a personnel specialist, two jury clerks, a financial administrator, the Clerk of Court's secretary, and a number of former supervisors who suddenly found themselves without a clear role. Over time, we added a second personnel officer and an architect/project manager for a new courthouse we are building. We – and they – had mixed feelings about whether they constituted a team or not.

These individuals shared a common mission of support services to the operations end of the court, but performed distinctly different functions. Due to the need for internal controls and a separation of duties in the handling of money, let alone the types of expertise required for such varied responsibilities as budget management and personnel administration, the generic model of cross-training and backing each other up was not a good fit.

On the other hand, the notion of all of these individuals just hanging out there alone, in a team-based office with no supervisors, was no longer a good fit for the organisation. Therefore, our initial requirement was that these 'odds and ends' staff participate in the teams start-up workshop and design some mechanism whereby they would fit into the office's new organisational structure.

There was initial resentment on the part of many of these individuals at being asked to fit themselves into a team mold that they didn't think suited them. First they decided they were one team of overlapping circles. Then they decided they weren't a team, and temporarily disbanded. Then jury and financial split off as a team due to physical proximity and some overlapping of skills. The remainder of the group renamed themselves the 'Leftovers Team.' Then the Leftovers disbanded because they didn't think they were really a team. Later they regrouped and renamed themselves the 'Unteam.'

And now?

In the years since, the Unteam has become one of the most dynamic and exciting parts of our office. Precisely because their span is so broad – everything from courthouse space design to budget projections to personnel initiatives to the operational expertise of the former supervisors – they play a unique integrating role within the larger organisation. They are in the forefront of recognising new technological solutions and initiatives, anticipating their impacts on operations, and identifying resources for implementation. Other teams in the office tap into their expertise and assistance for training and internal consulting, pick their brains as part of teams' problem-solving, and use their project management skills in keeping large multi-team projects on course.

A few examples might be helpful:

1. We recently implemented a new program whereby court orders are scanned into the computer and faxed to the attorneys. This saves postage, provides speedier notice of judges' decisions to counsel, and relieves docket clerks of the time-consuming tasks of copying, folding, and stuffing orders into envelopes. A multi-team task force consisting of docket clerks, automation staff, and members of the Unteam visited other courts to observe a variety of different automation techniques and operational processes for accomplishing this.

   The cross-functional task force, including automation and docketing, decided the best model for our office. Members of the Unteam coordinated the purchasing, organised task force meetings and took minutes. They pre-tested the equipment and connections, and identified for automation staff the numerous docketing details that would be affected. The team did outreach and PR activities with the local bar, processed attorneys' authorisations and entered their fax numbers into the computer, provided quality control to ensure that faxes were successfully transmitted, and much, much more. The two groups most directly affected by this large-scale project made the fundamental decisions, but it's hard to see how they could have handled the myriad of details necessary for implementation, in addition to their regular daily work, without the assistance of the Unteam.

2. Our office recently developed an Internet site for attorneys and the public, and an Intranet site for internal use. Again, representatives from the affected teams participated in a task force to plan, design, and implement this project. Automation staff coordinated linkages to the Circuit's 'firewall,' set up modems, and handled the technical aspects. Operations staff provided the ideas for content and, in every instance where it was practical, maintained the material. For example, the intake clerk who produces our civil case list also updates and revises the list in Lotus Notes for the Internet and is responsible for its accuracy and timeliness. Members of the Unteam received training in Lotus Notes and Domino in order to create and revise templates for these materials, tested the links to ensure everything continued to work, monitored the feedback from the public, and created new linkages and sub-sites for easy use by the operations staff.

3. One former supervisor, now a member of the Unteam, was very concerned when we first converted to teams. She possesses excellent skills in a broad range of operational, computer, and analytic areas, but was very unsure of how they would or could be used in this new environment. In the very earliest stages, the teams tended to focus inwards and keep all 'outsiders' at arm's length because of an extreme sensitivity to anyone encroaching on their self management. That made it difficult for this ex-supervisor to create effective linkages with the teams who could best use her skills. In time, the teams became more confident and relaxed about

their status, and were no longer afraid of appearing weak if they asked for her assistance.

Today she's pulled in more directions than she can handle, and if I could clone her, the office would be well served. She still has all of the operational expertise from when she was a front-line supervisor, but now combines that with new computer skills she's gained through specialised training. She develops sophisticated programs to streamline routine tasks performed by front-line workers, is much in demand as a trainer, and is routinely asked to participate in team projects. The moment of validation for her came when we recently proposed that she move to another corner of the office so we could convert her existing space to some other use. She balked, and indicated that she would have to talk to her 'customers' because her existing location was along a convenient pathway used by the operations staff. In speaking to each of the teams she works with they laughed and assured her that she was so valuable to them that there was nowhere she could go in the office that they wouldn't track her down!

But this isn't the end of that story. While the Unteam is flourishing, the other part of that 'odds and ends' group, the jury and financial staff who call themselves the Administrative Team, is not doing so well. This team presently consists of two jury clerks and two financial administrators, but it is in reality two 2-person teams. The financial administrators have distinctly different ideas about proper workload distribution and quality control in the financial area, and the problems arising from their stalemate have become extremely disruptive. The jury clerks do not accept this as their issue, and have not intervened to help resolve the problems. Despite all of our attempts to resolve this situation informally, no progress is being made. At this point we are sending both administrative support teams – the Unteam and the Administrative Team – to a new participative design workshop for the purpose of re-thinking how to organise administrative services so that all functions are part of a healthy team or teams. If there's one truism we've found with teams, it's that nothing is cast in concrete. We're constantly evolving in the face of changing circumstances.

When Teams Fail

Let's not be naive, not every team succeeds at its first attempt at self management. One of our teams, Intake, began floundering a couple years after becoming self managing because of turnover and some poor decision making choices. When Intake showed no signs of being able to pull itself out of its downward cycle, we knew we had to intervene in a most direct way.

The Intake Team is responsible for: processing mail; opening and assigning new cases; receipting for funds received in the mail and over the counter; managing the court's records and the movement of closed files to and from the off-site archives; and dealing with the public who are filing papers or viewing files. The team generally serves as gatekeeper and receptionist for the court. Additionally, each intake clerk has individualised desk duties including appeals docketing, processing of prisoner complaints, management of the miscellaneous caseload, and maintaining the automated case list.

Intake is an entry level position for the office, and had recently experienced turnover. At the same time, some of the existing intake clerks decided that they wanted to switch desk assignments with that of some of the vacated desks. The result was that, with a single exception, all staff were new and untrained in the tasks they were performing. This problem was compounded by the fact that they were using each other as trainers, and in many instances the person doing the training had only fragmented knowledge about the subject matter. Their desks and general work area were cluttered and disorganised, important papers were misplaced in all this mess, and what manuals and resource materials they had were impossible to find in all the clutter. Due to inadequate training and hurrying too fast, their work was characterised by an excessive number of errors which was impacting everyone else in the office.

The atmosphere at intake was unprofessional, with staff shouting across the room at each other, eating at their desks in full view of the public, and often treating customers poorly or in an overly familiar manner. And within the team there was real anarchy. Team members simply announced when they were taking the day off – no one asked or even considered how many other people might also be off and whether there was adequate coverage or backup. No one felt it was their place to criticise another team member, and even if they did, no one on the team felt that anyone else had the right to tell them what to do anyway. There was lots of griping behind each other's backs, but no one was direct and honest about it. The most experienced intake clerk broke down under the pressure of trying to hold it all together and was out of the office for weeks at a time under doctor's orders due to high blood pressure. Such was the situation when we in management decided that this team simply could not pull itself out of its downward spiral without outside intervention.

We began our intervention with a meeting between the Management Team and the Intake Team where we gave them a memo detailing our observations and stating our intent to take over the supervision of the team for a period of three months. Our stated goals were to provide resources from our own management team and the Unteam to give them job-specific training, help them organise their work areas, help streamline their procedures through automation and more efficient work processes, give them telephone and customer service training to improve their professional image, and show them by example how to give and receive honest feedback. The intent was to restore them to self management in three months.

We employed a variety of techniques to accomplish this. We started with in-depth interviews with each of them regarding how they perceived the problems of the team, what outcomes they sought, and what role they thought they could play in moving the team forward. The write-ups of these interviews were shared with all of the team. Later on, we concluded our three-month intervention with formal evaluations of each of the team members, as well as an overall evaluation of the team itself. These materials were also shared with all team members.

Very early on we conducted a detailed time study and showed them how certain of their processes were working at cross-purposes with the rhythms of the day. For example, the mail clerk didn't receive the mail until 11:00 or 12:00 noon. She took her lunch from 11:30 until 12:30, so she usually started processing the mail (which took her about two hours) after lunch. That meant that it wasn't until 2:30 or 3:00 in the afternoon before the day's mail got distributed. The daily mail normally contains a large number of checks which have to be receipted for, which also meant that one of the intake clerks was trying to complete the day's receipts just when the afternoon rush was reaching its peak. We worked with this clerk to stream-line her mail processing so it only took an hour, and discovered that by her walking one block away to a mail staging area, she could pick up our mail by 10:00 and have it completely processed before lunch. That meant that the receipt-writer, by taking a late lunch from 12:30 to 1:30, could complete his receipts during the slow noon to 1:00 time period. The whole office therefore had their mail by noon, and the receipts were completed long before the afternoon rush. We found several such small adjustments that made intake clerks' lives easier.

We also used the Unteam to provide comprehensive training in all of the functional areas the intake clerks were responsible for. In the process, Unteam members helped intake clerks make better use of automated tools and reports, eliminated unnecessary steps, and helped them sort through their notebooks and papers to throw away the outdated material and label and organise the resource materials they needed.

We forced intake clerks to slow down at the counter, by making them go through a week of 'shadowing.' During each clerk's 'shadow' week, only two of them were allowed to handle the whole intake counter – all other clerks were removed for specialised training. The clerks were 'shadowed' by experienced intake clerks from the other divisional office or members of the Unteam, who expected them to stop and explain what they were doing with each item of business they were conducting, and why. This, of course, led to long lines at the counter, not only because they were forced to slow down, but also because there were only two staff handling what four or five usually handled. They hated it, but each learned techniques for blocking out distractions and focusing on the papers they were processing rather than panicking over the lines. And our observations of customers sticking their arms across the counter to shove papers at them and trying to catch their attention while they were in the middle of a transaction led us to install a rope barrier like airlines or banks use to keep customers in an orderly line and a few feet away from the counter. After that terrible week, the normal rush of business didn't panic them nearly so much and they were able to keep their composure – and their accuracy – during the busiest normal times.

During this three-month intervention, each deputy had to schedule at least a half-day with a trainer or member of the Unteam to learn better PC skills, particularly how to organise their word processing and e-mail records, and how to use an automated calendar and organiser system to which the whole team had access. At the end of this training, many of the intake clerks had better PC skills and more customised set-ups and macros than most of the rest of the office, which helped restore their confidence. They were also required to set aside at least a half-day to clean up and organise their desks, paying attention to clear labelling. All produced a 'map' of their work stations so that in their absence their backups could find what they needed. This alteration of their physical environment also had an effect on their work performance. Additionally, we scheduled training in customer service and telephone skills. All joined in a discussion about what 'professionalism' meant to them and how they would demonstrate it in their work.

Probably most importantly, I met with them each and every morning for 15-30 minutes to give them feedback on the previous day, discuss what was pending on everyone's desk, coordinate schedules and activities, and confront issues. Both positive and negative feedback was given publicly, so they could see that it was okay to comment on each other's performance. One 'sacred cow' we confronted was saying no. On occasion I denied requests for time off, which was something they had never done before. They learned that it was possible to put office needs ahead of individual wishes and still retain good relations with the person being turned down.

The lowest point of our three-month program came about two months into it. Bruce and I had to go out of town for several days, and upon our return we learned that in our absence things seemed to deteriorate at intake – no early morning meetings to coordinate the day, more socialising, and no one showed up on time for scheduled telephone training. We met the next morning, with all members of the team defensive and offering excuses for why they had been late. Bruce responded that their focus on individual excuses was evidence of the lack of cohesiveness of the team and would hamper their ability to ever succeed. He said that one alternative for us was to simply turn them loose, tell them they were now self managing, and if they failed then he'd replace them with people who *could* handle self management. Or they could come up with some alternative. But we were at a loss at how to proceed. They'd learned their specific job functions, but we saw no signs that they'd progressed in their ability to manage themselves. After a *very* long silence they agreed to think about where we go from here and to meet with me early the following morning.

That seemed to have been the turning point. By the next morning every member of the team had a list of specific suggestions for how they could responsibly manage their team. They had culled material from previous training sessions, stayed late at work to brainstorm, prepared written points, and made commitments to each other about how they planned to implement these ideas. 'Results Not Excuses' became the motto of the team. There were no more serious setbacks after that point, and by the end of the three month period the team assumed the responsibilities of self management.

This team remains, in general, the most inexperienced team in the office due to its positions being entry level. But today they have high morale, are among the most active participants in training and office committee activities, have successfully brought in two new people of high calibre, are very supportive of each other, have excellent communication, and perform their jobs with distinction. This difficult time truly bonded them as a cohesive group.

What do we see ahead of us? One of our most exciting new prospects is the building of a whole new courthouse in Seattle. Like most organisations, we are presently housed in a facility that no longer fits our values or ways of working as a flattened team-based organisation. We still have private offices, denoting status and separateness, which we can't afford to remove. And most staff work in cubicle-type workstations which share the dual problems of not being private enough for concentrated work, nor open enough for collaborative teamwork. Neither arrangement has the flexibility to allow teams to have the types of spaces needed for the variety of tasks they perform. The building of a new facility from the ground up gives us a unique opportunity to create an environment, which reflects and supports our new ways of working.

We began the space planning process with structured focus groups consisting of the team members. People explained how they work, who they work with, what adjacencies they need, what equipment and support services they require, and which elements of their existing space and furniture support their work well and which pose problems for them. We discovered that all teams perform three distinctly different types of work:

- ♦ 'Heads-down' or concentrated work which necessitates freedom from distractions
- ♦ Interactive work involving collaboration and access to others
- ♦ Process-type work involving routine task completion

While process-type work (whether docketing, financial, personnel, etc.) could be accommodated with either a well-done private office or systems furniture, concentrated work and collaborative teamwork require very different environments. The solution is to recognise that every employee and every team need a variety of work spaces to support the range of tasks they perform. Everyone needs options to choose when they need to work in private areas and when they need an environment of stimulation and openness. Today's furniture and technology support these needs. All the following and more are available for designing an environment that supports self management:

Laptop computers, wireless keyboards, 'smart' whiteboards that can be downloaded into a computer and shared via a network, adjustable and portable furniture, variable-height dividers on wheels, tackable walls, cellular phones, 'caves' (private spaces for concentrating) and 'commons' (interactive team space).

We're also paying attention to the flow of traffic within the office to encourage spontaneous communication across team lines. I don't know if I'll succeed in getting my internal boulevards with coffee bars and café tables, but that's what I'm striving for!

As we get further into the design process, we plan to take team representatives out to observe other office environments, as well as to trade shows and display showrooms to show the range of possibilities that exist. We hope that what we end up with is something that uniquely suits us and how we work.

Our teams are constantly evolving. Check back with us in a couple of years; we hope to have an even more interesting story by then!

Janet Bubnis and the teams at the Western Washington U.S. Clerk's office are featured in the Federal Judicial Center's video documentary, 'Team-based Management,' produced by Blue Sky Productions.

E-mail: Janet_Bubnis@ce9.uscourts.gov

Chapter 13
Orchestrating Success

by John Lubans

In music, the term **conductor** conjures up Wagnerian and Toscanini-like images: temperamental, gifted, iron-willed, and not a little despotic with their musicians. This daunting image is pervasive in the music field and makes a conductorless orchestra as unlikely a notion as a business without a CEO. Without the conductor's absolute control a symphony would devolve into discord, or so we think.

All the more surprising then is the unrivaled success of a musical company that has never had a conductor.

The Orpheus Chamber Orchestra is a company of 26 elite musicians, founded two decades ago by cellist Julian Fifer. Orpheus creates a superb sound *without* the direction of a conductor. And, they regularly win their industry's highest awards and play to full houses at Carnegie Hall. Orpheus is the meshing of highly educated and accomplished people doing a 'simple' thing, playing music, pursuing the Orpheus trademark 'unanimity' of sound and 'clarity of expression'.

This successful ensemble offers rich lessons for managers in any type of business, but especially for leaders of loosely knit, creative organizations of equals. Many start up companies formed in recent years can benefit from observing Orpheus. Like Orpheus, these new organizations are nimble, unconventional, goal oriented, collaborative in nature, and maybe out to show the traditional corporate world a thing or two.

But, as these start ups mature and grow in size, organizational structure becomes increasingly important. With more people, compartmentalization and formalization of processes, complex communication systems, and shareholders looking for a return on investment, the 'how' of organizing can no longer be an afterthought. It no longer suffices to claim, 'we're just like a family'. Organizing becomes a conscious and deliberate application of a strategy in order to achieve a mission.

While the hierarchy rules the organizational landscape, some managers believe that the hierarchy represses creativity, collaboration, and team work. In fact, much of what may have made the first few years of a start up exhilarating and fun, with everyone eager to come to work, could be inhibited by the institution of a hierarchy. How then to keep that creative sparkle, productivity and joy working? There are alternatives to the hierarchy, but do they work?

The Orpheus Chamber Orchestra is a successful example of a self managing strategy that can be applied to any organization. The Orpheus model offers much more than another way to organize a business. They stand out in decision making and giving feedback to each other, and in their ability to collaborate, genuinely.

Lessons from a rehearsal

The Orpheus Chamber Orchestra makes its home in New York City near W. 120th at the Riverside Church, that bee hive of social welfare activity, near Columbia University. On the 11th floor, the sign on their open door is whimsically reassuring to the out-of-town visitor: ORPHANS Chamber Orchestra.

In the rehearsal room, where windows on one side overlook Riverside Park and the Hudson River, the orchestra is forming and tuning up. Amidst the cacophony, Norma Hurlburt, Executive Director, explains the Orpheus tenets:

Orpheus has a simple mission, to perform a great concert, perhaps a 'perfect concert'.

Interaction in rehearsal is essential, with civility valued as an 'operating norm'. Since you may be the next concertmaster (each piece has a different concertmaster, so responsibility rotates through the orchestra), respectful and responsive behavior serves everyone well. The concertmaster, the 'first chair' inside the innermost semi circle, leads the group.

Accountability is immediate and absolute. With no conductor, the performers have no one to blame but themselves if they do not achieve *their* goal.

Membership in the Orchestra is decided by Orchestra members, not management.

Management does not impose its 'vision' on the musicians – Orpheus is set up in a two headed model of musicians and management. This twenty years-old model consists of a self governing orchestra that deals with music decisions and, on the other side, the Orpheus Board and staff that manage the career of the orchestra and get the money to make the enterprise run.

For every dollar of income gained from a performance, there is a dollar of subsidy from other sources; a healthy ratio for orchestras. Orpheus does not exist to make money; rather, Norma says, semi-facetiously, they seek 'to lose money in as prudent a way as possible' – Orpheus has a different kind of 'bottom line'.

The 'cores' (small groups that discuss notation and interpretation of the segments of any concert) have helped introduce efficiency so rehearsals are speedier, no longer the reputed three times longer than a 'normal' orchestra might take. The concertmasters and players indeed pay an exacting attention to time; this economy is obvious also in the brevity and precision of feedback.

The group, some twenty this morning, commences to rehearse an early Mozart piece for performance at Carnegie Hall.

A remarkable sound fills the room; from the first precise notes, an observer can tell they are very good. The listener, present to observe the group's dynamics, is in danger of becoming totally enthralled by the music instead.

The music flows, rises, falls, pools, and flows again. The interplay and the manner in which players give feedback are readily apparent. Their verbal exchanges, like their music making, is marked by a direct linearity, a simplicity of expression that leads to a clarity of understanding among the players. Their dynamics of collaboration can be boiled down into something as fundamental (and yet elusive in the corporate setting) as these elementary school 'class discussion rules':

♦ There are no dumb questions or dumb answers.
♦ It's OK to say I don't know.
♦ Keep asking until you really understand.
♦ If you don't agree, say so, and explain your thoughts.
♦ Teasing, put downs, and sarcasm are not allowed.
♦ You have a right not to take part in discussions.
♦ Don't criticize people – agree with or disagree with their ideas.
♦ It's good to have a mind of your own.

All of these norms become manifest in an Orpheus rehearsal; they underlie and drive how the players talk to each other.

The group self corrects, verbally, as it plays, penciling in changes on individual scores. Feedback is frequent, seasoned with humor, and diplomatically given.

There are no dumb questions or dumb answers. Comments/feedback comes from all over the arc-shaped rehearsal seating, not only from the actual players, about their parts or roles. Players comment on the sound, the quality, the interpretation of the entire piece. There's awareness that this is *their* product, not the concertmaster's. Because of this sense of ownership, collaboration is intense.

Talking about music requires a vocabulary akin to language used to describe qualities of food or wine:

'Not too meaty'.

'Too pale' someone says.

'Coloration' is defined and redefined.

Sometimes, vocalizing the score, the way it sounds and the way it *should* sound, works best of all.

It's OK to say I don't know. Someone asks the group, 'What do I need to do to make it work better?' (This remarkable request calls to mind the quip about the three things managers are still NOT taught to say: *'I don't know', 'I made a mistake',* or *'I need help.'*)

If you don't agree, say so, and explain your thoughts. One of the two French horns, at the end of the piece played straight through, admonishes the group, objecting to the overall sound: 'Don't do this to me, people. HE (Mozart) wanted it *that* way!'

Keep asking until you really understand. Another player, a cellist, whose initial comment fell on deaf ears, speaks up again, repeating her criticism, asking, 'Is that bad?', i.e., does my comment have substance or not?

Dead center in the rehearsal arc, in the conductor's 'zone', stands a miniature conductor doll in a red velvet box on a music stand. The concertmaster had made a point of tapping on the stand with his bow, like a conductor demanding the group's attention. It is a joke, but there is an underlying subtle reminder that this is not how they operate.

At the same time, the concertmaster and others agree that strong conductors, even despotic conductors, are OK as long as they have talent/vision. Not OK are those conductors who want to use their orchestras to 'talk about it', as if their own lack of direction can be fulfilled by group discussion.

Now a different piece (Grieg: *Two Elegiac Melodies*) and a new concertmaster, a woman:

Polite. There is immediate good interaction, but there is a perceptible difference. Some deference to, or is it carry over from, the Mozart concertmaster, a male? She leads in a different way, a smaller orchestral group with several players gone. About half way through she has established her low-key style as 'leader' for the piece.

After lunch, at 1:15, the orchestra swells to 35 musicians, including a harpist, oboists and a trombonist, to do Copland's *8 Poems of Emily Dickinson*. There is to be a vocal soloist. It is said to be a hard piece.

They begin; the vocalist reminds the orchestra of the 'seriousness' and the intended tone of the poems. Copland desired to imitate musically the spoken word.

It's good to have a mind of your own (and use it when it matters). The new concertmaster for the Copland piece is circumspect; she'd been poring over the score during the lunch break. An unusual dynamic comes into play – while the concertmaster is subdued, others fill in acting as supporters, interpreters. The most vocal one had had very little to say during the morning, now she takes the lead in reinforcing what the concertmaster is saying.

'Can we try the strings a bit faster?' after a long pause and discussion.

Keep asking until you really understand. 'I don't know when...' the soloist talks to the entire orchestra about the poem, 'Going to Heaven'. Side conversations erupt. (Is that where the work gets done? In group dynamics, this is something to avoid – the splintering of the group – yet, here it seems to be working towards solutions, the musicians clarifying individual points among the winds and strings). The orchestra repeats the poem again, and again, and again. The vocalist stops at several points along the way, not satisfied with her phrasing or the musical sound.

It is now 2:35pm, and the 'Going to Heaven' piece is moving, the sound is rolling, rising and falling in perfect pace and pitch with the voice. They make it! Congratulatory smiles abound!

So, what does a morning of observing Orpheus mean for the work place?

The experts tell us that people have some basic 'wants' from their jobs. If the wants are met, the theory goes, people will work at a higher level than when they lack any or all of these:

♦ Adequate elbow room for decision making.
♦ Opportunity to learn continually on the job.
♦ An optimum level of variety.
♦ Mutual support and respect.
♦ Meaningfulness.
♦ A desirable future.

Orpheus appears to exceed all of these 'wants' with the possible exception of the 'desirable future' – economic forces are pressing on some orchestra members and many often hold other income-producing positions, usually in conventionally organized orchestras. That aside, Orpheus' liberating environment encourages the type of feedback and interaction necessary for high performance. At the risk of stating the obvious, every organization of human beings would probably like these 'wants' met. That they are met in the Orphean world with superlative outcomes should strongly encourage any executive to pay attention to these 'wants' in his or her business.

The successful manner in which Orpheus functions, the mutual respect and trust they display, their clarity of purpose, their 'unanimity of sound' are worth emulating in any organization.

At the same time, there is a sense of fragility about this fine creation, perhaps it is inherent in the beauty of what they do, in the loveliness of the music that they make. It is like a quixotic dream that could evaporate after twenty years of success.

The orchestra is, in fact, stirring, reinventing itself in 1998 into a new Orpheus:

The musicians who seek a greater voice in their future and want greater economic returns for their work are pushing for change. The early days, when it was not unthinkable for a musician to play for free, for the joy of making music, are days

gone by for Orpheus. An 'environmental scan' would reveal a perceived 'threat': namely, that the classical music world is shrinking, all the rage for the 'three tenors' notwithstanding.

There is an 'opportunity' in the orchestra's maturity. They are poised for growth as they enter their third decade, ready to move to a new plateau. Interestingly enough, the Orpheus self-study, after over 20 years of existence as an organization, coincides with the S-shaped growth and decline curve theory. The enhanced prestige from being named 'Ensemble of the Year for 1997' by the classical music industry underlines this strength and is a capstone to Orpheus' career to date, symbolizing a need to move on to the next level, catching the upward curve, or risk an inevitable decline.

From the intense and, at times, emotional stakeholder discussions, it's becoming clear that Orpheus is more than the musicians. All 45 of the Orpheus administrative staff, board members, and musicians are bound together by a love of music, and each brings special gifts (music, fundraising, creativity, marketing, organization) to the process. As members reflect on their common purposes, respect and understanding appear to be growing. The love of music does transcend numerous differences and difficulties – it is the dominant reason that Orpheans want the enterprise to survive.

What will make Orpheus' new organization more than just another corporate re-shuffling? What will make it a true metamorphosis and not mere adaptation to current trends? Besides the quintessential love of music, there are two centripetal forces:

A sense of decency in the organization. Decency is the word Norma Hurlburt uses to describe the values underlying what everyone is seeking for Orpheus. The concept is that organizations can be decent places to work.

The respectful and honest exchange of ideas. The orchestra excels at the giving and taking of constructive criticism to improve its performance. There is every reason to think this quality is a corporate norm. The ability to confront and creatively adjust ought to help shape a new organizational order at

Orpheus, one palpably different from the current model, moving to a new, higher level.

Reflecting on Orpheus, it seems that the words of St. Augustine apply to them and to other organizations struggling towards a model of self-governance, in pursuit of new and greater levels of organizational achievement:

> *In essentials, unity,*
> *In non-essentials, freedom,*
> *In all things, charity.*

Addendum

I am back, on a cold February day, in New York to hear Orpheus play in the nave of the Riverside Church near West 120th Street at one of their community concerts. My seat is close to the front, at the altar where the orchestra, buffered by acoustical frames is to play, with Pepe Romero, guest classical guitarist. Several hundred people await the music to start.

The day before I met with Norma Hurlburt, to talk about Orpheus' future. Since she resigned her Executive Director position in July of 1998, I have had an opportunity to speak with her and the new Executive Director, Harvey Seifter. Norma remains committed to the Orphean ideals of a musician-regulated organization, bonded together by a love of music and through that synergy, to create a sound of incomparable beauty. Orpheus continues to change – under Harvey Seifter's leadership there is a heightened emphasis on bottom line concerns, a firming up of what might have been regarded as loosely-knit. Orpheus founder Julian Fifer is continuing in the role of President & Founder.

The musicians settle in on stage and the music fills the church. I am again delighted in their product as three different concert masters take their turns and put their own leadership stamp on each section. The depth of the interaction between them and Mr. Romero is a joy to see. As I revel in the moment, I recall Norma's comments from yesterday that, now, when Orpheus is at its best, it draws upon the depth and refinement of maturity and years of hard work with one another. In their early days, she observes, they had an energy and excitement driven by their youthful desire to take the world by storm – which they did!

Today, like any mature organization that passes through a golden age and begins to change and to grow, Orpheus faces the ongoing challenge of 're-invention'.

John Lubans (March 11, 1999)

(An abbreviated version of this chapter appeared in United Airlines *Hemispheres* magazine, January, 1999, pp. 44-48 under the title, 'Orchestrating Success: Case Study')

Orpheus *plays at Carnegie Hall.*

The orchestra resides at:
490 Riverside Drive,
New York, NY 10027.

Phone: 1-800-ORPHEUS.
Web: http://www.orpheusnyc.com/

John Lubans *is a senior manager at Duke University's Perkins Library. He has consulted in executive development programs at Duke's Fuqua School of Business and writes frequently on management topics and the Internet from a user's perspective.*

Fax: 919 660 5923
E-mail: Lubans1@aol.com
Web: www.lib.duke.edu/staff/orgnztn/lubans/john.html

Chapter 14

Do-it-yourself Management at Do It All

Martin Large with Mal Tanner

In this chapter, Martin Large describes Do It All's courageous struggle to become a self managing workplace. Do It All is a company that operates retail stores in the UK for customers wanting do-it-yourself products and services for the home. This story dramatically illustrates the problems an organisation can experience when it tries to implement self management in a top down fashion. How DIA recovered from a shaky start has rich lessons for anyone considering redesigning to self management.

> 'They used to be on your back all the time, telling us to do this, do that, checking up on us every five minutes, these were usually young assistant managers fresh from training!'

This was how Michelle Barton, who has worked at Do It All's Lichfield store as an assistant for ten years, described the old way of doing things. 'Now, things have changed totally since we redesigned the way we work in 1997: we have time for customers, they give more compliments to us, and even ask for you personally when they come back for more help. The managers are part of our team now, we are treated with respect and equality, there is no fear any more and I can tell them what I think.'

She enthused about working hard, and how the four in her team rotated through each area for a month, so they knew each product well, and how standards and store profits were rising. She spoke with obvious pride about the importance of paint finishes, the merits of frosted glaze, how her feedback had got into the company bulletin, and how she was looking forward to giving feedback to a visiting marketing manager on customer needs and questions.

According to Mal Tanner, former head of personnel and training, participation works. Do It All had been suffering severe losses of £98 million in 1996. Formed in 1990 from a merger between Boot's Payless and W.H. Smith's Do It All, the chain had to close 80 stores and reduce the workforce from 6500 to 4500 because of over capacity in the DIY (do-it-yourself) market and the housing slump.

One secret of getting into the black lay in the implementation of a thoroughgoing approach to participative working, to do-it-yourself management, using self managing teams. According to former Personnel Director Geoff Kidd, 'This is a journey. We're a few steps down the line, and there's a way to go. I remember asking, how do you enable participation to happen where at the time it was clear there wasn't any participation or involvement at all?' And for Mal Tanner, 'The DIA story is about learning, about moving step by step, about people learning where they are and where they want to go: an organisation acting, reviewing, learning and then acting.'

An overview of the journey towards a self managing workplace

The DIA journey started with a company wide coaching programme that aimed to melt down the prevailing autocratic command and control culture. Coaching resulted in limited business improvements, so self management was introduced in the stores. And whilst workers like Michelle Barton liked participative working, it was still basically a bureaucratic structure with a human face. For example, she said there were still team leaders, the managers were part of the team.

Mal Tanner realised the instability of this 'half way house', particularly with operations managers wanting the security of the old system. There was a real danger of full reversion to a bureaucratic structure. So he then tried to shift DIA to a completely new self managing structure in which workers redesigned their own work, deciding on team composition and responsibility. And he was working to help operations managers design their work teams, when DIA was bought by Focus in August 1998.

The improved DIA results are evidence of the success of participative working. Within eighteen months, DIA had the best customer service standards, (BT/Daily Telegraph Awards), the lowest staff and manager turnover, and one of the lowest shrinkage figures in the DIY industry.

So what were the stepping stones on the way? What success was achieved? For example, whilst DIA introduced participation, did this stop short of a self managing workplace? And the learning?

Establishing a distinctive Do It All Culture

There was a strong command and control culture, as described so well by Michelle Barton. Geoff Kidd called this 'management by lists', as exemplified by 'the store visit' by the regional manager: 'Right, bring me your book, we're going round the store. I don't like that, please change that. The gondol needs changing, that line control hasn't been put in, do this, do that.'

The store manager is walking behind writing all this down in his book. At the end of the walk around the store, the regional manager says, 'Right, sign here. I'll be back at the end of the month to see if you have done it.'

Poor business performance led DIA in 1993 to establish a business strategy which focused on improved customer service, new merchandise development, cutting loss making stores, improving IT and central distribution, and improving its image in the marketplace. Central to the success of this strategy was the development of a distinctive culture based on the following values:

- ♦ An honest and open working environment
- ♦ Employee participation and involvement
- ♦ Team working
- ♦ Encouraging creativity and innovation
- ♦ Risk not blame
- ♦ An enabling and a fun environment in which to work

Personnel manager Jacky Beesley discussed these values further, commenting that:

> 'The characteristics seen by DIA as arising out of these shared values were that this would lead to a risk taking culture which would enable employees to feel free to contribute to the business without the fear of being unfairly criticised or ridiculed. Everyone's view and contribution would be encouraged and valued. Fundamental to realising these values was the view that to enable employees to grow and develop their contributions to the business, management must adopt a leadership style that reflected delegation of power down to subordinates, listening to, and motivating employees in decision making.'

Coaching for performance

A coaching environment was created. It was thought that if managers became good coaches, staff would take more responsibility for their work, rather than just following instructions. The programme was designed by Nic Turner to enable a culture change from the prevailing autocratic to a coaching style of management. All six directors, senior managers, 600 head office staff and store managers went through a three-day coaching course. The coaching course was part of a change process that included upward appraisal within the regular performance reviews.[1]

As a result, the climate of fear and distrust began to disappear. For example, when directors visited stores previously, staff played the game, 'Let's see if we can survive the director's

visit by pulling in extra staff from elsewhere to create an im-
maculate store.' After coaching, the questions on such store
visits became: What's been going well? What's been difficult
since the last visit? How can that be done differently? What
feedback have you got for me? A newly inducted manager
commented that, 'This is the first company I feel I'm working
with my boss and not for him. I'm not told to do this or that all
the time.'

But coaching was not enough

In 1996, Tom Radford, the new operations director, triggered
the introduction of self management by asking Personnel why
coaching had not been fully implemented in the stores. 'Why,
after all this training is coaching still not embedded?' Whilst
DIA was minimising losses, profits were elusive, with staff still
task, but not customer, focused. Tom Radford wanted to replace
the widespread dependency on management, with staff taking
responsibility for real service through self management.

Another blockage to a coaching style was the strongly hierarchical store structure:

General Store Manager (GSM)

|

Store Operations Manager (SOM)

|

Sales Floor Manager (SFM)

|

Service and Systems Supervisor

This was backed up by a secondary hierarchy of store consultants
who trained and developed advisors and assistants. Advisors
and consultants were part of customer services, supported by a
different set of field staff and managers. According to Mal
Tanner, 'This group was almost separate from the sales operation. As a concept it was great having people in a store with a

high level of expertise. But in reality it just increased the levels of bureaucracy within the organisation. It also meant that other staff thought it was the consultant's job to improve service levels, so all they had to do was stock the shelves, not to talk to our customers.' So Mal Tanner and Tom Radford decided to introduce self management to address the fundamental issue of the location of responsibility.

Introducing Self Management

Self management was first tested in the Bromsgrove store, before being implemented elsewhere. One reason was that, according to Tanner, it was run by one of the most respected, but autocratic managers DIA had. It was also a successful store. Tanner briefed the store managers on self management, using only five pre-prepared flip charts, in order to test how suitable it would be for implementation by line managers. The GSM was at first not pleased at the implied criticism of her management.

Two weeks later, the team met again with regional personnel and training manager Jacky Beesley and were invited to redesign their own jobs within the broad outline of the new suggested roles, and to maximise their individual human needs using the six criteria for productive work. The guarantees to reassure managers included:

♦ No change to grading, authority, pay levels, or promotion channels

♦ Store managers to become contact coaches, engaging with staff and customers as opposed to spending most of their time in offices

♦ Operations managers, floor managers and supervisors work as a self managing team

♦ Staff, in three self managing teams, to own their part of the shop floor

'Within three weeks, the atmosphere between the GSM and the rest of the store management team was electric,' according to Beesley. 'Once they started working as a collaborative team, they didn't want to give it up. It improved their lives, inside and outside of work so much.'

The new store structure was changed to:

General Store Manager (GSM)

Team Leader — Gardening and Workshop

Team Leader — Decorative

Team Leader — Checkouts and Cash Office

Each of the three supervisors became team leaders and briefed their teams, who then came up with how they wanted to work. Sales staff now planned their work, deciding who is responsible for what sections. Instead of being supervised by job lists, they planned new sales promotions, talked with customers about new products, organised the team's holiday rota, developed in depth knowledge of products, covered for each other and for other teams. In some stores, staff selected new recruits from a short list.

This new way of working gave much more time for team leaders to clarify their work, because they no longer had to organise their staff's work. Indeed, at the Bromsgrove store, one of the most important things learned, according to Mal Tanner, was 'how much more competent the team of three actually were than they thought they were. When the GSM first moved from the store on secondment, the team decided they did not want another GSM. This was a dangerous area because it frightened the organisation. It was interesting that the store continued to get good results without the GSM there.'

Reflecting on this redesign process raises the following questions. Firstly, how much preparation is needed by, say a store manager, for redesign? It came as a surprise to the Bromsgrove manager. Time was needed to think and work through the principles with other store managers.

Secondly, the decision by Operations Director Tom Radford that the design should be three teams with leaders means that the use of a participative design workshop was ignored by the dictation of a design from top down. Usually, redesign starts from the ground up, and the workers may or may not have decided that three teams made sense, given the workflow.

Thirdly, there are still team leaders/supervisors who talk about 'their' teams in the redesign, which shows that no structural change has occurred, even though there have been many other positive changes. (Was control and coordination of work located with team members or the team leaders?)

And lastly, why was it 'dangerous' that the store management team performed well without a GSM? Could it have been that the three team leaders/supervisors, realising that the teams were perfectly capable of de facto self management, could then concentrate on overall store management? A conclusion from this could be that the old supervisory and new team leader roles were just not needed.

Implementing self managing teams in all DIA stores

Self managing teams were implemented via the company's regional managers, with a day workshop led by Mal Tanner. This gave them the opportunity to discuss and understand the differences between design principles, the bureaucratic and self managing workplaces, and how these affected the criteria for productive work. They then briefed their teams of GSMs who then briefed their store management team and then the staff. Each store management team rewrote their jobs and agreed tasks, and presented this to the GSM to sign off. All 157 stores implemented self managing teams by Easter 1997, within two months of testing out teams at Bromsgrove. All briefings and redesign work was done within each store, and within normal working hours. This was virtually a nil cost intervention.

This was a low cost, rapid way to introduce self managing teams, relying on a top down process of cascading change. There was the danger, given the company history of command and control, that such an approach could be criticised for sending such double messages as, 'participate or else!' Or 'let's participate our way.' It was also risky to rely on the widely different interpretations of self management that went out to the 157 stores via regional briefings to store managers.

So the personnel and training team worked over eighteen months to support the implementation of self managing teams through coaching the regional and store managers so as to make redesign work in each store. This support was understood as needed at the outset, and the regional personnel and training team became the implementation team, working as consultants to the managers.

Does self management work at DIA?

Self management at DIA works. For example, Mal Tanner described the big fall in labour turnover and discipline cases. 'We used to manage our staff by disciplining them. Self management has dramatically cut the number of cases we have had to handle. It has also reduced labour turnover, which has fallen every month for more than a year now.'

He puts this down to the fact that workers felt their human dignity was being respected. Also, they were more productive at work since redesign. All 4500 staff were surveyed in March 1997, and resurveyed six months later, showing marked improvements in 14 of the 15 questions. For example, there was an increase from 42 to 56% of people feeling their ideas were valued at work. However, the areas still needing attention were learning / feedback and desirable future. The external researcher com-mented that, 'Compared with the original figures, something major has happened. I am staggered because all the indicators bar one have moved significantly.'

Another result is an increased sense of ownership: 'When you come in to buy something and you come into contact with our staff, it is like meeting the owner of the store, and that has to be good for business,' says Mal Tanner. GSMs have more time for management with less time in the office. Their chronic overwork and stress became a thing of the past. But with hindsight, there was still much work to do.

Challenging the bureaucratic workplace: the organisation bites back!

The stores, now very keen to improve their performance, began to bring pressure on Central Operations to improve their response to store feedback. This triggered Central Operations wanting to align with what was happening in the stores.

At the Central Operations alignment workshop, however, Mal Tanner invited them first to clarify their overall purpose, since their existing mission was all 'motherhood and apple pie'. Because a cross section of managers and staff attended, there was considerable challenge to the existing ways of thinking and doing things. The managers prided themselves on being customer focused but this was challenged by a secretary, 'It was a lovely spring day, I walked into a DIA store and I couldn't understand why there was such huge display of loft insulation at the front of the store? Surely that's for the autumn or winter?'

She was told that she did not understand about carriage costs, storage and so on. But she held her ground, 'As a customer, I don't want to know that. Why don't I see an attractive display of outdoor furniture?' As a result, Operations realised they were accepting bureaucratic decisions that were impacting negatively on the customers, instead of putting customers first.

As a result of the workshop, Central Operations implemented with the stores a complete feedback loop within three weeks of things that were working well, everything that wasn't working and things that needed improving. (The company had

talked about the need for such a feedback loop for two years
prior to the workshop, without anything happening.) At first,
there was a barrage of negative feedback from the stores, which
was difficult to take, but slowly the number of positive things
began to increase. Central Operations started to be creative and
outward looking. It became an energetic place to work, and
linked closely with the stores.

'My learning was that any part of the organisation if left to
itself will develop its own objectives and strategy with few links
to the business goals and the customer,' said Mal Tanner.
However, there were other signs that the old bureaucratic
organisation was biting back. For example, in head office,
product managers were becoming fed up with all the negative
feedback from the stores of things that needed fixing. They
found it difficult to understand that the store staff was
customer focused, and wanted their supply systems streamlined
so as to increase service levels. They also found it hard to
understand that all the feedback was contributing to learning
how to improve the ways they worked. So requests came to Mal
Tanner for a workshop to equip GSMs with the skills for giving
feedback more nicely. His response was to refuse, and challenge
people by asking, 'Is this request coming from the bureaucratic
or self managing principle of design?'

Colleague Jacky Beesley was also concerned about the
extent to which management style had changed after redesign.
Her survey results and recommendations led to Mal Tanner
devising a Redesign Review workshop for managers to respond
to the biting back of the old bureaucratic organisation.

To what extent has management style changed after self management?

By cascading redesign to regional managers, store managers
and junior managers and kicking off the process so quickly in
early 1997, there was the question of the extent to which
management style and behaviour had changed to enable
participative working. According to Mal Tanner, 'We kicked the

programme off fast, and got fast results, but we always knew there would be difficulties. We dealt with it by getting regional personnel and training managers to work with the general store managers on a one-to-one basis as consultants, helping them to develop strategies to resolve problems.'

Geoff Kidd described the problems some store managers experienced as 'a feeling of over delegation, of loss of control. The difficult thing for store managers, particularly with self managed teams, was the worry about losing control. They are very used to coming in the morning and saying 'Right, Bill you do this and you do that'. Suddenly it was all being done for them. And they thought well, what do I do? You have to remember that it is just one year since we started, but a number of them are now understanding their role as a contact team coach. So they actually spend more time coaching and more time with customers than they ever could under the old system. Interestingly, the turnover of managers has dropped substantially since we brought in self management. So maybe they are finding the job more enjoyable with less pressure on them.'

Six months after the implementation of self management, Jacky Beesley researched the extent to which management style and behaviour had changed since redesign. She was interested in the fact that maintaining previous managers as the new team leaders might undermine participative team working. DIA had assumed that because of their extensive coaching training, the new team leaders would positively demonstrate the behaviours supporting self managing teams and optimal scores for the six criteria for productive work.

She found that after six months in 40% of stores, team leader behaviour supported effective participative working across the six criteria. But for the other 60% of stores, there was a mixed picture, with team leaders both supporting and hindering participative working. So some team leaders continue to lead autocratically in relation to opportunity to learn/go on learning and variety, as well as meaningfulness and desirable future. At the same time, leaders were supportive of elbow room for decision making and mutual support and respect where contact was good.

Jacky Beesley's interviews with store staff and managers at this early stage show a mixed picture of participative working. For example, a store operations manager was asked, what do you think of self managing teams? 'I think they are a good idea but am not sure if they are working as they should, and of course we have less overall control. Also, some staff just want to be told and some staff don't understand the priority areas.'

And an assistant: 'I'm aware of them (self managing teams) but I'm not sure I've seen a lot of difference. Mind you, managers have management team meetings and they seem to be working more as a team to cover for each other. But it has caused issues of separation on the shop floor. I now only work in one area (rather than the whole store). Also, attitudes of 'it's not my area' are common now, especially by the customer service team. My product knowledge is shrinking as I don't know what's new in other areas, just my own. As it is, I don't think they are really working. We shouldn't have divisions; we should be working more flexibly to supply the whole store. But I'm not really asked for my ideas because I'm part time.'

These findings, not unexpected at this stage of a top down change process, helped the implementation team identify priority stores to work with. Jacky Beesley recommended that, 'Team leaders revisit the principles of self management and be clear about the differences between a bureaucratic and self managing work organisation to ensure they understand and take fully on board the need for their behaviours to be discontinuous.'

There were also increasing requests to the incoming head of operations for detailed guidance from store managers about their jobs. This led to the design of a workshop aiming to deliver detailed job outlines (job descriptions in disguise) plus levels of accountability, from staff through to regional managers. There were pages of instructions for store managers to follow as coaches, and a regurgitation of the original self management notes in a simpler form.

This plan shocked and astounded Mal Tanner because it was such a clear indication of the bureaucratic organisation biting back: 'When I recovered from the shock, I realised that the beliefs of the organisation, including my own function and members of my own team, were still attached to bureaucratic design. Thus, my own function, personnel, was unwittingly colluding with operations to provide a bureaucratic 'cure' for the natural and expected growing pains of participative working methods.

'Fortunately, I was able to persuade Tom Radford, the Operations Director, to stop this wrong headed intervention. This decision produced a very angry reaction from the head of operations, regional managers and my training colleagues. However, I had finally realised that the original roll out of self management had been introjected by operations and my department in the usual bureaucratic mindset of dependency; dependency on the expertise and knowledge of the supervisor, *me*. Thinking back, how could it have been otherwise?

'So we devised Redesign Review workshops for all regional managers and regional personnel managers, before having them run it with store managers. The guidelines for the workshop were:

♦ No more theoretical or expert input

♦ Explore the discontinuities in thinking, feeling and behaviour in the bureaucratic and self managing workplace design principles

♦ Create real dialogue on the paradigms of bureaucratic and self managing design

♦ Learn to learn from each other, rather than from the supervisor

'Written information about self management was given as background beforehand, together with notes on the rapidly changing business context in which the DIA changes were happening. The workshop started with participants doing a scan of changes in the world important for DIA's future, which were triggering the need for radical, discontinuous changes in how DIA worked. This was followed by sharing the story of DIA. The real challenge was participants understanding the fundamental differences between design principles. It was scary, energetic and noisy, as long held beliefs, values and attitudes were challenged with the question, 'Which design principle is that coming from?' Participants then worked on their understanding of self management, the criteria for productive work, the skills matrix, and then shared their progress and plans in their stores.

'The workshop focused on experiential, group learning so as to break the dependency of being fed or instructed by the supervisor. A key element was to encourage authentic dialogue to surface, to question deeply held or unaware beliefs and attitudes.

'The learning for me was that the original implementation of self management did not allow for dialogue to create new beliefs and behaviours to replace the old ones. This almost resulted in the return of the bureaucratic organisation!

'However, there is a paradox in helping people move from bureaucratic to participative working. No amount of education before introducing self management into organisations would ever be enough in itself to create the change, and it requires experiential learning for its successful implementation.'

Current position and results

The Redesign Review workshops successfully made up for the problems caused by the original cascading of self managing teams. By revisiting the principles, 'Lights clicked on for a considerable number of managers.' Jacky Beesley continues, writing that, 'For some managers this was the first time they had really understood that you cannot behave in an autocratic management style in an adaptive work environment. I would definitely incorporate this as part of introducing participative/collaborative working on future occasions.' The Reviews helped consolidate the critical mass of managers who modeled and championed participative working.

The business results of participative working, however, were favourable: eighteen months after implementation, DIA achieved the best customer service standards, the lowest staff turnover and shrinkage figures in the DIY industry. But we will never know how the DIA story would have turned out. DIA was in the process of redesigning its stores to full self management when the company was sold by Boots in August 1998.

What can be learned from the DIA story?

The overall culture change process used at DIA began with the training of coaching skills as a way of moving beyond command and control. This prepared the ground for the introduction of self management. However, even though participative working was introduced, DIA was only just beginning to take on the challenge of becoming a self managing workplace.

There was the continual tendency for the bureaucratic organisation to bite back, for example the resistance to the feedback from the stores to central operations. From a bureaucratic perspective, this was negative, and should have been couched in 'nice' terms. From a self managing perspective, such feedback could be seen as learning, as a temporary wave that would subside once systems and processes had been streamlined. Store feedback would then increasingly concentrate on increasing service and value to the customer and supporting front line teams.

The 40/60 split of stores wholly supportive of self managing teams to those giving mixed support as identified by Jacky Beesley in her Autumn 1997 survey can be seen as a result of not changing the structure to self management. It was a 'half way house'. To the extent that there was participative working, this was unstable, with the danger of the tendency to revert to the old command and control way of doing things. The stores that had managers who understood the implications of self management were always bound to be supportive of self managing teams. One could argue that a good proportion of the other store managers neither understood self management nor implemented self management. Their stores were self managing in name only. Whilst shop floor staff were keen on participative working, a proportion of managers were less sure, fearing loss of control, loss of their traditional job of management by lists.

Many managers and workers understood very well what self managing workplaces were like, and the differences with the reality of their coaching, team leader run workplace. For example, several store staff mentioned in interviews how, 'we just put up with the coaching from team leaders, since these managers knew so little about how the work was actually done.' And even though these workers were *told* they were self managing, they knew they were not there yet.

Mal Tanner made the point with clarity, realising that the original 1997 roll out of self management had been re-interpreted and absorbed by operations and personnel into the usual mindset of bureaucracy. So this realisation then triggered the 1998 Redesign Review workshops to challenge such thinking and embed the shift to self management.

There were, of course, already many examples of stores well on the way to self management. For example, in Bromsgrove, the group of team leaders had temporarily managed the whole store in the absence of the store manager, thus allowing 'their' teams more space for self management, and preparing for a more desirable future for themselves.

Another reflection is the discovery of the importance of challenging assumptions and practices using Mal Tanner's question, 'Is this coming from the design principle of the bureaucratic or self managing workplace?' This enabled people to see which of the two paradigms were at work.

With hindsight, a full-scale participative redesign would have allowed store staff to redesign the self managing structure themselves, instead of the top down prescription of three teams. There would have been the choice to either absorb the previous supervisors or managers into self managing teams, or to enable them progress to other jobs rather than get in the way. However, Operations insisted on a cautious approach right from the start, and therefore Personnel were constrained by what was achievable. (Hindsight is a wonderful thing!)

In contrast to the extensive coaching workshops, the original redesign was economical of time, fired people up, was rapid. Also it was owned by DIA Operations rather than Personnel and was not dependent on expensive consultants. But the rapid, cascade implementation was also problematic, in that many managers and workers from the outset did not understand the real differences between the bureaucratic and the self managing design principles. So a lot of follow up work had to be done before the lights went on.

One critical issue raised by the DIA case is the fundamental difference between the human relations approach to participation, and the self managing or second design principle. The human relations approach to participation originated in Elton Mayo's Hawthorne experiments, in which teams of workers who were specially selected and supervised became highly motivated. Participation came to mean securing worker compliance through communication, positive relationships, feeling special, making decisions on peripheral matters and experiencing satisfaction at work. So the human relations approach to workplace redesign emphasises the importance of coaching and participative working to reduce the effects of the command and control, bureaucratic structure. On the other hand, the self managing design principle (*real* participation) involves workers designing their own work, so they are in charge of coordination and control. This generates the commitment, motivation, energy for effective work and the resulting satisfaction.

So, starting with a thorough going participative design workshop approach could have allowed store staff to redesign the self managing structure themselves, instead of the top down prescription of three teams. Given the chance, employees would certainly have come up with alternatives to the three team structure mandated by management. And there would have been the choice to either absorb the previous supervisors and managers into self managing teams, or to enable them to progress to other more challenging jobs. As it was, DIA took a longer way round, first trying participative working and then realising it was a 'half way house'. This triggered going with the

Redesign Review workshops to complete the transition to self management.

As Mal Tanner said, 'You cannot learn to swim without experiencing yourself in the water.' So if you want a self managing workplace, give people the opportunity to design it themselves.

E-mail: Mhclarge@aol.com

E-mail: maltanner@compuserve.com

Chapter 14
Do-it-yourself
Management at
Do It All Stores

Chapter 15
The Market Alignment Imperative

Gary Frank

As Monty Python liked to say, 'Now for something completely different!' Well not really, but this next chapter offers a fresh way of looking at organisation design at the level of the whole organisation. It's meant for senior executives who manage large-scale organisations. If you're an executive who is attracted to self management, but wants to start with a strategic level of design, you will find Gary Frank's ideas right up your alley. The lessons you can learn from this chapter apply even if you are leading a large public sector or government organisation.

This chapter is about organisation design at the level of the whole organisation. A 'whole organisation' is a large-scale enterprise with multiple divisions such as marketing, manufacturing, research and development, and more.

Whole organisation design requires a different conceptual model and a different design principle. The conceptual model is the 'open system' and the design principle is the 'market alignment imperative.' The chapter will develop the aspects of the open systems model relevant to organisation design, introduce the market alignment imperative, and illustrate how one organisation used the design principle in its redesign.

Medical Instruments

The year is 1996. It is late March. The place is a conference room of a major manufacturer of medical instruments. Sitting around the table are senior managers, directors and vice presidents, from headquarters and field sales, product and procedure marketing, and human resources. The discussion is about the current alarming business situation. The revenue and profit picture for the current quarter is significantly off plan. A bleak quarter close is upon them and the prospects for the second quarter are equally grim. The atmosphere in the room is a combination of confusion and deep concern. The questions are these: What is happening? What went wrong?

Since the company's founding in 1991, Medical Instruments' (an alias used here to protect the real company's identity) rise in the market place has been meteoric. From being the new upstart, Medical Instruments has risen steeply in market share and revenue. In fact, by its fifth year in existence, it topped the $500 million mark and assumed market leadership from its chief competitor. Now, in its sixth year, sales are suddenly flat and those at the highest corporate levels are beginning to ask questions.

In 1991, when Medical Instruments was founded, it was organised, like any organisation at the time of its founding, around certain marketplace conditions and corresponding assumptions. Four conditions characterised the healthcare marketplace in the United States at that time:

1. The marketplace was still highly local. Medical knowledge and technology aside, what was happening in the Miami market had very little to do with what was happening in the Seattle market.

2. A fee-for-service environment prevailed. A fee-for-service environment is characterised by two conditions. First, medical insurance benefits function almost like a voucher that can be redeemed at any doctor's office. Second, patients/consumers therefore act as free agents taking

advantage of their benefits and seeing pretty much any doctor, including specialists, they wish. There are, of course, guidelines to be observed and paper work to be submitted, but whom the patient sees and when is almost entirely at their discretion.

3. Low penetration of managed care in the marketplace. Managed care organisations like Kaiser Permanente were present nation-wide, but did not dominate the healthcare landscape.

4. In a highly local, fee-for-service marketplace with low managed care penetration, the physician ruled. In particular, in a hospital setting, the surgeons ruled. This meant that the surgical staff determined what procedures were used and what instruments and supplies were purchased.

Given this set of market conditions, Medical Instruments used the following criteria to guide its original organisational design.

♦ In a marketplace that is and always has been highly local, design the organisation to reach localities.

♦ Since the marketplace is local and uniformly distributed, subdivide the marketplace without regard to regional or area differences.

♦ In the market, a fee-for-service market prevails and surgeons rule. Design the organisation to treat the surgeon as the selling target.

Medical Instruments designed itself to be successful in this marketplace. It hired a clinically experienced sales force and focused their efforts on building relationships with and influencing surgeons locally to practise certain procedures that use Medical Instruments' equipment. It organised and deployed its sales force geographically (regions, districts within regions, and territories within districts). It took its annual plan and divided it evenly among the regions to arrive at each region's contribution to the total revenue goal. It centralised all other functions at headquarters leaving a pure sales focus in the field.

Medical Instruments flourished for nearly five years with this design. But in 1996, things began to go wrong; the beginning conditions had change substantially. While the great healthcare debate in Washington consumed media attention in 1994 and 1995, a revolution was in fact reshaping the healthcare landscape. By 1996, managed care had penetrated much deeper into many more markets. Managed care in the form of health maintenance organisations (HMOs) had become a household term. Large managed care organisations, such as Columbia, were gobbling up independent hospitals at an astonishing rate and establishing huge national networks. Fee-for-service environments continued to exist, but it was becoming clear that the marketplace was becoming more, not less, differentiated.

Perhaps more significant, power had shifted. New roles in managed care organisations, such as chief financial officer or purchasing manager, were assuming power. The 'primary care physician' became the gatekeeper to something called the 'care pathway'. In general, physicians, once the locus of power and control, were feeling disenfranchised; those who paid the bills and tended the bottom line were calling the shots.

So, in March of 1996, a room full of senior managers ponders two questions. How do we get a handle on this? When we do, what do we do about it?

Environment as the Critical Context for Organisation Design

Medical Instruments, Inc. is like lots of organisations. Perhaps you see your own organisation in the story. The story is true at some level for almost all organisations. Start-up conditions and assumptions change. What was true five years ago is no longer true in the present. But, so often, nothing about the organisation's fundamental design changes. Its basic architecture remains the same even if it no longer responds to the conditions and features of the marketplace. Much effort is usually put into patching up the existing organisation: technology is updated; processes are re-engineered; quality programs are instituted; compensation and incentives are changed; new talent is recruited to bring new vitality. And although these are all reasonable and often necessary changes, they are mostly insufficient to address the root cause; the organisation is out of sync with its environment. Like an engine that is badly out of tune, it labours inefficiently to keep going.

But these conditions needn't persist. An organisation's overall design is variable, to be changed and leveraged the same as other variables, such as technology, process, compensation, and the selection of key personnel. An organisation's original design is not a condition that must be endured or worked around. Its architecture is a key variable that can and should be changed choicefully to its advantage.

To help us think about how to design an organisation that is in sync with the conditions and feature of its marketplace (and keep it that way), some concepts are particularly useful. These concepts are the 'open systems model', 'organisation domain', and 'task environment'. These concepts will lead to a new design principle, the market alignment imperative, and the outline of a fresh approach to whole organisation design.

Open Systems. Fred Emery described a conceptual model that is a useful way for thinking about organisation environments. The figure below depicts the model.

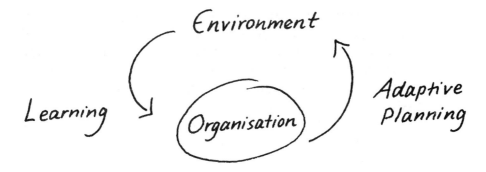

The open systems model illustrates the features that are important for understanding organisation-to-environment dynamics and ultimately whole organisation design. All organisations operate in the context of a larger environment. The environment in this model is everything outside the organisation's boundaries. All organisations interact with their environment. The nature of the interaction is particular to the organisation. There are obvious material, capital, and information transactions or exchanges, but there is special kind of interaction that is an important feature of open systems. It is the interplay of influence between the environment and the organisation

If the environment is the organisation's context, then its influence is broad. The environment determines conditions like availability of capital, access to materials and markets, how densely or sparsely populated the market place is with competitors, and more. In most cases, the environment influences the organisation much more than the organisation influences the environment, although that is preferable.

As the model illustrates, the environment-to-organisation dynamic is about learning. The key question for this aspect of relationship is what is going on in the environment that the organisation must understand and to which it must respond successfully? Conversely, the organisation-to-environment dynamic is about active, adaptive planning. Given the set of circumstances the organisation has learned about, what must it do to maximise its opportunities and insure its survival? So, influence is a key form of interaction.

As we begin a new century, any organisation's environment is less uniform and tending toward greater and greater uncertainty. This is what Fred Emery and Eric Trist called 'turbulence'. To the extent that the environment is becoming (or has become) turbulent, the level of organisation learning and active, adaptive planning in response must match that turbulence.

Organisational Domain. Two concepts that work in combination help to shape the environment further. The first is the concept of organisation 'domain'. All organisations must establish a domain. An organisational domain is a claim that an organisation establishes for itself regarding its range of products, the population served, and goods or services rendered. For example, Medical Instruments established a domain that includes the production of videoscopic surgical instruments and education in their application and specific use in hospitals and out patient medical clinics.

Task Environment. There are parts of the environment that are particularly relevant to goal setting and goal attainment, and therefore, organisation design. These parts are referred to as the task environment. The task environment is composed of four generic sectors:

♦ Customers
♦ Suppliers of material, labour, and capital
♦ Competitors for markets and resources
♦ Regulatory groups, such as government agencies and unions

As we learned from Medical Instrument's dilemma, massive changes were occurring in the task environment. Everything from the nature of the customer to the political terrain was shifting underfoot.

If the concepts of open systems, organisational domain, and task environment are combined, the organisation's environment becomes clear and actionable. An organisation can design its overall structure to be adaptive and successful in its market.

The Market Alignment Imperative

A new design principle now comes into focus. The design principle is the *market alignment imperative*. The name conveys the importance of an organisation's most important motivation, alignment with its market. Market alignment is not something that falls into the realm of 'nice to have,' or 'wouldn't that be good if we have time.' It's an imperative. It is among the most important things an organisation can do.

The market alignment imperative states the following:
Design the basic architecture of an organisation to provide maximum alignment with the most salient demands of its market.

Organisations must create themselves in the image of their market. Customers are looking for partners who are easy to do business with. They are looking for organisations that understand their challenges and requirements, can help them respond to those challenges and requirements, and are accessible. To the extent that they see themselves reflected in another organisation's operation (derived from its choice of structure), they will find that organisation attractive as a business partner.

While the notion of aligning with customers or having a customer orientation *is not* new, the idea of designing your organisation's structure fundamentally and specifically with your customers in mind *is*. Again, many organisations have done cosmetic work in this direction without having changed their basic architecture to assume the features of the market. While they may experience some improvement and advantage in this way, the improvement and advantage are not as substantial and effective as they might have experienced had they gone the distance and truly aligned themselves to their market.

Designing the Whole Organisation Using the Market Alignment Imperative

Designing organisations at the level of entire enterprise using the market alignment imperative is not light work, but then the importance is not lightweight. Whole organisation design is a comprehensive, systemic intervention intended to recreate the organisation to align with the imperatives of its market.

Scanning the business environment. The preceding discussions of the environment as critical context for organisation design and the market alignment imperative should have made abundantly clear the importance of doing a thorough environmental scan. It is important that any organisation learn as much as it can about the external trends, forces, events, and developments that are influencing its very existence. Environmental scanning is best accomplished by engaging in dialogue with the key stakeholders that comprise the organisation's domain and task environment to identify the requirements, demands, and opportunities placed on it by these stakeholders.

Several important questions structure this dialogue:

- What is the nature of our current relationship?
- What is your experience of your current relationship with us?
- Where do you think your business is headed in the next three to five years and what will that mean for our relationship?
- How must we change to accommodate your changes?
- What's the best supplier/customer relationship you have?
- What makes it such?

The wisdom of experience teaches that multiple sources and multiple approaches yield the most useful and complete information. A good first step is to read trade journals, newspapers, books, and magazines and attend meetings and conferences to develop a basic orientation to the demands and requirements of the market. The second step is to engage directly with stakeholders. This may happen in several ways. One way is to do one-on-one interviews with key representatives. A second way is to conduct focus groups with stakeholder cohorts. Or a third, powerful way is to invite stakeholders to join organisational members in real-time dialogue and exploration of their relationship and the future in a forum like the search conference.

Further, these approaches can be used in combination. The purpose of scanning is to build market knowledge; it can also build relationships. If done with systematic rigor, the results are potent. The organisation becomes smart and connected to its market in ways that it wasn't before.

The results of the scan can be translated into design criteria. Design criteria are a set of statements that capture the essence of the environmental scan activities. An example of design criteria was mentioned earlier for Medical Instruments: 'Design the organisation to reach localities.' A successful whole organisation design must respond strongly to as many criteria as possible. Once the design criteria are written, whole organisation design can begin. The first step is the creation of a basic framework or architecture for the organisation.

(The creation of a whole organisation design requires design activities that are beyond the scope of this chapter. However, because organisation design is how the market alignment imperative is operationalized, the creation of a basic organisational framework or architecture is the foundation of the design.)

Building the organization's architecture. Whole organisation design fundamentally comprises the following tasks and decisions:

1. A critical examination of current business activities to determine which to keep, which to drop, and which to add in relation to what was learned in the scan. This is often referred to as a boundary question. What will be inside versus outside the organisation's boundary? The organisation's current menu of business activities may no longer be appropriate to its reconsidered purpose.

It may be that something the organisation does now no longer fits the picture portrayed by the scan and should be dropped. Or, it may be that something the organisation does now can be done cheaper and better if it is outsourced. Or it may be that the organisation does not do something now that it must if it is to align with its market in the future.

Medical Instruments, for example, determined from its scan that it did not know enough about local market conditions and resolved to deploy additional market analysis and market development capacity to the field organisation. The result of this critical examination is a menu of business activities that fits the organisation's purpose.

2. The second step is the most critical. It's the designation of a basic configuration for the new organisation. A configuration is a structural shape the organisation will assume in response to its market. This is where market alignment is operationalized. Organisational configuration is based on an overall organising principle. Authorities differ on this matter, but there are basically five pure organising principles. An organisation may be configured according to:

    ♦ Function
    ♦ Product
    ♦ Geography
    ♦ Customer
    ♦ Process

These methods of organising may also be used in combination. This results in a hybrid configuration. For example, an organisation may choose to have both a functional and a geographic configuration, i.e. certain functions that are geographically distributed because of geographical differences in market.

The key question is, 'What configuration aligns our organisation most closely with requirements and demands of our market?'

3. The choice of a basic configuration for the organisation results in logical groupings of work by organising principle, e.g. functional groupings, process groupings, customer groupings, etc. These groupings must be defined in terms of purpose, composition, tasks, and activities. These definitions are crucial, macro-level descriptions of how the organisation is intended to function.

4. Lateral processes to integrate and coordinate the organisation's activities. Any amount of differentiation must be reintegrated. Lateral processes are those organisational mechanisms by which people working in different structural components (logical groupings) communicate, share knowledge and information, make decisions, and become whole

to consider organisational issues. Lateral processes are not such things as voice mail, e-mail, electronic bulletin boards, memoranda and the like. They are structures, specific roles, or work arrangements that cause people in work groups either to be face-to-face about matters of mutual concern or to pay attention to each other's activities and requirements. They may be such mechanisms as:

♦ Liaison roles – identification of specific people who act as an information conduit between groups.

♦ Cross-functional groups – temporary or permanent groups of representatives from all the functions who come together for a variety of purposes from problem solving to product or service delivery.

♦ Integrator roles – non-management individuals who have an integration oversight responsibility for several separate groups.

♦ Matrix structures – the deployment of functional resources (e.g. marketing, technical support, customer satisfaction, etc.) to product, customer, technology, or process teams for the purpose of bringing that expertise to the team.

Whole level organisation design does not end here. The new organisational units should be defined and designed further. Jobs, roles, and relationships within and between units are defined. Processes, procedures, and work arrangements are all examined, refined, or redesigned and tested. Support systems and mechanisms should be developed to align with the intent of the new organization. People need to be selected and trained for new jobs and roles. And a strategy for implementing and managing these design and change activities is developed.

If the design principle at the whole organisation level is the marketplace alignment imperative, the design principle that guides design at the next level or levels is the self managing workplace principle: locate responsibility with people who do the work. So, the next step after whole organisation design could be to do participative design workshops throughout the entire organisation, using the new boundaries and groupings as the framework.

Don't be put off if you are an executive in a public sector or government organisation and you are wondering how a concept based on markets applies to you. Regardless of the type of organisation, any organisation must be designed in alignment with its environment to be successful. Instead of customers, welcome your important external stakeholders in for a dialogue about what is happening in the environment from their perspective.

Medical Instruments Aligns with its Market

It is April 1996. After considerable internal discussion to diagnose the situation and explore alternative courses of action, the effort to address Medical Instruments' sagging sales begins in earnest. The effort is dubbed Target 2000, in the expectation that the new design will be successful by the year 2000.

The managers decide the importance of the effort demands their direct involvement. Rather than appoint a project team, they decide *they* will function as the oversight and project team and enlist the help of others as project demands require. In a series of early meetings, they develop a project plan and they develop an initial vision of their desired end-state for the project.

The project plan calls for extensive scanning and a thorough organisational diagnosis. The scanning effort will use multiple approaches. A market analysis currently being conducted by an external consultant will provide important background for the project team. A significant new report about the healthcare environment published by a respected think tank will complement. Interviews will be conducted with thought leaders and consultants whose associations and practices cover the healthcare market. Interviews will also be conducted with CEOs, COOs, and CFOs of large managed-care organisations and hospital consortia. Focus groups will be conducted in each region of the country with physicians, consumers, and hospital and healthcare managers. Finally, internal staff will examine existing sources of data to identify customer trends and patterns in the application of videoscopic surgical procedures. These activities span the months of June and July.

All of the scanning data are important. However, the focus groups have the most impact. Multiple focus groups are conducted in each region with subgroups of the project team assigned to a region. Each focus group is a cohort – surgeons, primary care physicians, healthcare managers, and consumers. In their own words, they tell powerful stories about the changes in the healthcare sector. The dynamics of the changes in healthcare begin to crystallise in specific, personal, and powerful ways. The stories give life to the learnings from the other sources.

In mid-September, 1996, the project team is prepared to integrate all of the analytical data. They set aside one week offsite to consume and review the data from each analysis, to integrate the data, and to develop design criteria. The first two days of the meeting are devoted to consuming the data from multiple sources. On day three, the work turns to data integration. There are four key questions:

1. What are the major themes?
2. How do the themes relate to one another?
3. How can we characterise the marketplace?
4. How can we characterise our organisation's strengths and weaknesses in the marketplace?

Day four is devoted to developing design criteria. This is the hardest work of the week. Ultimately, 14 criteria are written and agreed to by the group. The criteria include the following:

♦ Design the organisation to be able to deliver products according to the differing needs of different managed care customers.

♦ Put responsibility for customer service in the field, close to the customer.

♦ Make product education a centerpiece of the new design.

♦ Locate market analysis in the field to allow for different local information gathering.

The review is careful to insure that the statements are rooted in the data. On day five, they develop a plan for next steps, including feedback of the criteria to headquarters and field units.

The project team convenes again one month later. The design work yields two viable models. One model has product segmentation as its organising principle. The second, like the current state, has geography as its organising principle. However, in this model, the geography is much more granular. Four regions are reconceived as six to ten (or more) smaller areas aligned with important geographic segments of the market. The areas are conceived as business units with profit and loss responsibility. A major shift in emphasis from a headquarters centric to a field centric organisation is conceived. Parts of headquarters marketing are forward deployed to the areas to provide front-line market analysis and strategy. A market development function is created as a support to all areas. This function's job is to work with large managed care organisations to help them understand where and how the use of videoscopic surgical procedures will help to achieve better patients results and manage cost. Upon assessing the two models against the 14 criteria, the second model – the new geography model – is a clear front runner and wins everyone's support.

At this time, all areas are operating under the new design. Personal testimony indicates that the new organisation has delivered on its promise. But the real proof is in the performance. While it is very difficult to partial out the effects of an intervention like an organisation redesign (owing to the inability to control for other variables such as new product development, autonomous market growth or decline, new regulatory requirements, etc.), the performance results are indeed impressive. In 1998, Medical Instruments increased its sales revenue by $100 million. It anticipates repeating that performance in 1999. Its Target 2000 goals look well within reach. Medical

Instruments appears well positioned to capitalise on the opportunities in its marketplace now that it has worked hard to align itself with them.

People
In
Charge

Gary Frank is an independent consultant and visiting lecturer at the University of Colorado College of Business Administration. A consultant with more than 19 years experience, Gary's work focuses primarily on guiding clients through major systems changes to create high performance work systems.

E-mail: gary.frank@worldnet.att.net

Chapter 16

Stories From Workplace Redesign Experiences

Nancy Cebula

In this the closing chapter, Nancy Cebula presents real life stories about people courageously changing their workplaces to be self managing. It's all about managers creating responsibility throughout their organisations. And it's about workers forming teams that take charge of their own work. These stories illustrate why the self managing workplace is so important to the success of organisations of all kinds, for it can unleash the potential of people. Workplace design is everybody's business – workers and managers. In these stories you see people participating in the redesign process, learning democratic skills as they go. Kurt Lewin said it this way, 'Democracy cannot be imposed upon a person; it has to be learned by a process of voluntary and responsible participation.' Enjoy these stories and then get started turning your own organisation into a self managing workplace.

For several years I have been consulting with organisations that want to put people in charge of their work. I have been privileged to be present while hundreds of people have redesigned their work to be self managing. Leading redesign workshops has become one of the highlights of my consulting career. I would like to share a few of the stories from my experiences.

Once, when finishing the first of a series of redesign work-shops in one organisation, all with the same agenda, my workshop co-manager, an internal staff person, asked, 'Won't this be boring by the fifth time we do it?' Even though the design of workshops in various organisations contains many of the same elements and activities, leading redesign workshop after redesign workshop has never been boring. Each group of people brings their own unique energy and perspective to this process.

Here are stories from various redesign experiences. The settings vary widely: a hospital; the Land Bank of South Africa; a hi-tech manufacturing plant; a nursing home; a major U.S. newspaper; and various units of the U.S. court system, including bankruptcy courts, district courts, and federal probation offices.

What I hope to share is the transformation I have witnessed. Groups of people have stepped up to the challenge of taking charge of their lives at work, both collectively and individually. As one young woman put it so eloquently, 'They (management) are giving us a chance to be managers – let's do it. And let's do it well.'

Hope

During the redesign of a branch of the Land Bank of South Africa, I saw one of the tea girls, Hope, staring and frowning at the skills matrix. (A tea girl was an employee of the old Land Bank whose work is to serve tea and coffee to the other employees of the branch.) When asked if she needed any help, she replied that she did not know if she should acknowledge her accounting skills on the matrix as she was a tea girl, and black, to boot. She had been studying accounting at night school and took the job at the Land Bank in the hopes that she could someday become an accountant. However, she was 'afraid' to mark the skills matrix in the accounting skills section. After a bit of encouragement, she put a check mark in several of the accounting skills boxes and hurried to her seat at the back of the room.

Two days later, when the employees were determining who should be a member of each team, the people on the accounting team discovered that they were short of one person. When they looked at the skills matrix to see who else might have some accounting skills, they discovered Hope's check marks. After a bit of discussion, they announced to the rest of the staff that they had solved their team member shortage problem and publicly invited Hope to join them. It took a bit of encouragement from many others in the room, but Hope finally got up and walked over to her new team.

Hope was a bit concerned that she had only studied accounting and had never worked at it. Other accounting team members promised to help her with training and support as they understand that this is the first time that she will able to use her skills and knowledge in accounting.

Months later, I was visiting this branch and saw Hope, sitting at a big desk, with a calculator and all the accoutrements that an accountant needs. One of her team members told me an interesting story. As the Land Bank had not finished changing its pay system, everyone was being paid the same wage they had earned before the redesign. So, Hope was being paid as a tea girl, several thousand Rand a month less than the other accounting team members were. When the branch was given its end of year bonus money, the accounting team voted to give all of their bonus money to Hope. They felt she earned it.

THE LINE

THE LINE is an engineering marvel found on the floor of a high tech manufacturing plant in the U.S. It was the epitome of the manufacturing assembly line. THE LINE had commanded that all work processes and team design revolve around its massive presence. There existed in this plant a myth that THE LINE was an immovable object that could not be modified.

One day, during a manufacturing redesign workshop, one of the design teams, a table full of assembly line workers and an engineer, were discussing better ways of organising how they do work. The discussion had on several occasions run up against THE LINE. Finally, one worker, in an exasperated tone of voice, said, 'If it weren't for THE LINE, we could really get organised better. Production would be smoother and faster. Jobs would be more interesting.' The engineer looked up, from a rather pensive pose, and replied, 'So, why not change it?' This was greeted with a few startled laughs, a few 'No way, we can't change THE LINE' remarks. Then the design team realised that she was serious and began redesigning THE LINE around the work of the team.

The other design teams were so impressed with this team's redesign of THE LINE that they jumped in and all worked together to create a successful new manufacturing environment. Instead of one line, with segmented pieces of work, now there were four lines, each making an entire product. A fifth line was devoted to developing the best process to make new products. It was run by assembly line workers and engineers, in conjunction with research and development. Management liked this new design and worked with the employees to implement it. THE LINE was reconfigured by the combined efforts of manufacturing and engineering, with a minimum of cost and down time.

Cross training was implemented so that each worker learned all the skills necessary to produce their team's product. Quality improved, production time was shortened. Customisation of products was easier to do on the new lines, so customers were very pleased with the plant. As new products were moved into production, manufacturing was ready, as the new product line had already been working with research and development to design the best manufacturing process for that product.

In the Nursing Home

While in a redesign workshop in a skilled nursing facility, a group of nurse's aides made a startling discovery. When they took a look at how work flowed in their unit, focusing on how they cared for the residents under their care, the group decided to map out a typical day in the life of a patient. When the third shift, the ones who work through the night, listed their activities, looks of 'horror' were seen, cries of 'I had NO idea' were heard.

It became crystal clear to them that they were waking the residents up about every two hours to perform various tasks: medications, vital sign checks, laying out tomorrow's clothing, bowel and bladder checks. Work had been designed with the convenience of the employees, with rather segmented work. One aide would go around the unit and check vital signs. Another would go around and lay out clothes. Another would do medications, and so on. People who worked during the day had complained that the residents were uncooperative, tired, grumpy, lacked energy for activities. Now they knew why.

At this point in the workshop, this group of nurse's aides decided to experiment with designing the work around the residents. They set up a system where they would try to wake the residents only once, unless a medical condition required more frequent monitoring. As a result, most residents were awakened once a night for vital sign and bladder checks, clothes were laid out, medications administered if needed. Management agreed to let them implement this change that very night.

The reports from the day shift were encouraging. Residents were far less grumpy, ate better breakfasts, were cooperating with staff, and were participating in more activities and with more enthusiasm. The night shift nurse's aides reported that their work was actually easier, even though they were still doing the same jobs. Because residents were only awakened once, they were more cooperative with the nurses aides so the work went smoother and took less time. And, what was especially important to the staff, they felt that they had made a significant contribution to improving the quality of life for residents in their facility.

Human Resources in a Hospital

When the Human Resources Department in a Midwestern U.S. hospital lost its director, the rest of the HR staff asked their vice president not to hire a new director. They requested that they be allowed to hire two new HR staff people with the salary money. In return, they committed to doing all of their current work plus the work of the director in a more effective and efficient manner. As the hospital was going through the redesign process to move to a self managing workplace, the vice president agreed to their request.

Prior to the redesign workshop, an employee survey was commissioned so that the HR department would have good information on how their customers felt about the HR service delivery. The results showed that they were not meeting their customers' needs in several areas. As a result of this survey, one of the HR department's outcome expectations became to be more responsive to their customers. Other expectations included their successful handling of the former director's responsibilities and that work would be satisfying and enriched for all HR employees. In this vignette the focus is on the work of the former director and how it was managed.

During the redesign workshop, the group took an in-depth look at the work that the former director was responsible for. In addition, the vice president participated in the workshop, so her expectations for the director's work were in the room. The HR team decided that the former director's work could be divided into five skill and knowledge areas: primary contact (for the HR team), driving meetings, mediator, training, and budget. They chose team coordinators' roles and rotation cycles, developed measurable goals, and a training plan for each of these areas.

For instance, one team member will take responsibility for budget coordination for one year, as that is the budget cycle at the hospital. This person will be assisted by a budget coordinator in training, so that there will be adequate skill and knowledge for the next budget cycle. In the mediator area, two coordinators will work in six month cycles. The team felt that the mediator work can be very draining emotionally; having two coordinators and a shorter rotation cycle will help ease burn out. The primary contact coordinator will do this work for one year and will sit in meetings called by other teams and the vice president, and will be the contact point for people needing to contact the HR department. The training coordinator will rotate every year, again reflecting the hospital's annual training cycle. The driving meetings coordinator will rotate every six months and be responsible for coordinating internal meetings.

People will receive training, if needed, prior to becoming a team coordinator, to ensure that adequate skill and knowledge is available to do the work well. One goal of the team is for every team member to be able to perform all five of the coordinator roles over time.

Newspaper Advertising Department becomes Self Managing

When a major U.S. newspaper decided to use a team approach in its advertising department, they chose to use a participative redesign method to put people in charge of their work. Each advertising team was designed to do all of the work needed to deliver quality advertising to their customers. This included marketing, sales, accounting, creative design, and production of the ads. In this newspaper, this was the first time that the production, sales, and administrative people were to work together on the same team.

The world of daily newspapers is filled with pressure, as people are faced with daily deadlines, customers who demand quality work, and increasing competition from other newspapers, as well as other media. The Internet is a fairly recent and major addition to the complexity of their world. The pace of work is very FAST and the pressure is INTENSE!

After the initial redesign of the advertising department, each of the new teams did a workshop to organise itself, using the Start Up Guide for Self Managing Teams (see chapter 8). The first team had responsibility for dealing with large, national advertising campaigns. This workshop was the first time that this team had met as a team. Time was spent learning about all of the work of the team and the skills and knowledge needed to get it done. The discussions about the control and coordination of the work were most interesting. These were people who had never sat down together to talk about what they do or how they do it.

241

Chapter 16
Stories from
Workplace
Redesign
Experiences

The team decided that they would be providing enhanced service to their customers if the people who were doing the creative work, the production work, and the financial work were able to talk directly with the customers. Traditionally, they had been in separate departments and had never had direct customer contact. Ways to cross train and share work was also discussed. Consideration was given to the fact that not everyone on the team would be cross trained in all aspects of the work of the team. Some of the work, for instance creative artistry, might not be a skill that all team members would learn.

The most interesting discussion came during the six criteria for productive work activity. The team was just starting this when in walked Sara, the advertising manager, their 'boss's boss'. She asked if she could stay a while and the team agreed. At first the team members were a bit restrained in their conversation about the first criteria, elbow room (autonomy). Then, when all the team members had shared their scores and what they felt about elbow room, Sara began to talk about her elbow room. She felt that she had way too little elbow room. In fact she had less than others on the team. They were very surprised at this. One team member said, 'And I thought life was always wonderful in management. Now I see that some things are better in my job than in yours.' This started a lively discussion that continued through all six of the criteria. The team members and Sara learned a lot from each other. The openness and honesty that flowed through this conversation enhanced the impact of the six criteria activity.

Re-Redesign

About six months after redesigning one of the branches of the Land Bank of South Africa, the branch director (BD) and the staff of the branch realised that they were in difficulties. Work was backlogged, customers were unhappy, cross training was on hold, and employees were under incredible stress. The BD called all of the employees together to try to figure out what was going on and how to fix it.

The employees and BD discovered that in the six months since the initial redesign workshop, many things had changed. There were several new products being offered, branch and team goals had been lost in the workload, recoveries of unpaid loans were not getting the attention they deserved, and there were hundreds of new customers wanting service. Many of these new customers were people who were historically disadvantaged in the old South Africa, including blacks, women, coloureds. During apartheid, the Land Bank limited its customer activity to white farmers. As a majority of the population of South Africa is black, when the new Land Bank opened its doors to the historically disadvantaged, many, many new customers came calling.

243

Chapter 16
Stories from
Workplace
Redesign
Experiences

In response to the conditions that had changed in the six months since the first redesign workshop, the branch decided to do a re-redesign workshop. The BD and the employees worked together to figure out the best way to:

♦ Divide the work so all customers could get service in a reasonable time frame;
♦ Make sure recoveries of delinquent loan payments proceeded in a fair and equitable manner;
♦ Deal with the backlog to shorten loan approval time;
♦ Set measurable goals for the branch and teams; and
♦ Take the time to cross train each other.

Rather than the cross functional teams that came out of the first redesign, now they separated out a team to specialise in recoveries, including people skilled in recoveries as well as people who were learning about recoveries. As the Land Bank makes money when people re-pay loans, this needed to become a priority. Other teams focused on loan processing, accounting, and the Step Up program and support work. In some ways, it appeared that the re-redesign was going back to the old way of organising work in this branch.

As one looks closer at this new four team structure, one realises that this branch did not go back to the old ways. Key differences are found in where the branch has located responsibility for control and coordination of the work. There are no supervisors in this new design. The teams have responsibility for making decisions about their work, they discuss different ways of doing things, they set goals and negotiate them with the BD, they manage their own quality, and they work across team boundaries, helping each other out when necessary. Loan approval decisions, formerly in the realm of the Head Office, are now made by a branch ad hoc Loan Approval Committee. This committee is made up of people from different teams, with people of different skill levels, so that newer people can learn about the intricacies of the loan approval process, yet still have the requisite skill and knowledge to make sound financial decisions. Membership rotates so that more people can become skilled in this area of serious responsibility and accountability.

The Land Bank also authorised using one hour of every day for training purposes by moving the official opening hours ahead one hour. This was a very powerful statement by the Strategic Management Team on the importance of training.

'Now I can use my brain at work'

This was a statement that I have heard over and over again at the new Land Bank. In the old Land Bank, blacks, in particular, were relegated to support jobs, such as cleaning and tea serving, regardless of education or experience. Now, people are able to use under-utilised skills they hold and develop new skills while moving into more meaningful work. As new, historically disadvantaged customers come into Land Bank branches, it is often the cleaners and tea servers who have the language skills to communicate successfully with them. It is the former cleaners and tea servers who can go out into historically disadvantaged farming communities to market the Land Bank's products and help customers with the paperwork.

'We have formed a corporation and are going to bid on the cleaning of the branch.'

Two people from the cleaning staff at a branch of the Land Bank have formed a legal corporation and have begun negotiating with the BD to provide cleaning services at the branch. They are very excited about this opportunity as it will allow them to build their own business as a cleaning services company. They are adding to their skills to make sure that they will have what it will take to run their own business, marketing, finances, management, etc. They are also excited about this new venture as they hope to find other cleaning contracts, expanding their own business opportunities and enabling them to provide jobs for other people. In a country with extremely high unemployment, it is amazing how many people are finding ways to provide jobs for others, one or a few at a time.

Many of the branch directors are exploring ways to help employees who are interested in working as contractors. As the head office focuses on key business practices, senior management is also looking at ways to facilitate outsourcing non-core work to employees who may be made redundant. Some of these ways include committing to lengthy contracts and giving the newly formed cleaning companies the equipment and supplies necessary to start up their businesses. Low cost loans may be available to help with other start up costs. Branch directors have also said they would help market the new companies within their local communities.

'In the first redesign, I was still a typist. Now I am learning how to process loans.'

Many of the women in the Land Bank have been traditionally employed as typists. As there was not an automated information system in place, all loan applications and documents had to be typed by hand. After the first redesign workshop, many typists were assigned to loan processing teams, as their work as typists would be eliminated by the implementation of the new

245

Chapter 16
Stories from
Workplace
Redesign
Experiences

information technology system. Due to the work overload, and some unwillingness to learn typing on some other people's parts (due, of course, to lack of training time) the typists were rarely able to leave their word processors as they were able to type the fastest.

Once the branch re-redesigned, one typist told me, 'I have gone from being a typist in the old design, to being a typist in the new design, to, finally, being a contributing and learning member of a loan processing team in the re-redesign. I had typed hundreds of loan applications and other paperwork in the past. Now I can work with people as they go through the application and approval process. I would rather use my head than just type what someone else has written. My future looks good now.'

'*I don't mind cleaning, but I really enjoy using my brain.*'

Another cleaner told me about his experience of being in the new Land Bank. He has had his matric (equivalent of U.S. high school) for several years, but was treated as though he was uneducated in the old Land Bank. Now, he and his team members have expanded the work that they do through working with the record/file room and the front desk, as well as cleaning. He reports that his team makes decisions about their work, coordinates with other teams, and negotiates goals with the BD. He especially enjoys working at the front desk, dealing with customers who come in, answering questions, and translating when they speak with others in the office who have not yet learned his language. He says that his work is more meaningful and he looks forward to working towards a spot on a loan processing team when he has built up his skills and knowledge, and an opening appears.

This story takes place in a U.S. bankruptcy court. During the redesign process, all of the supervisors became a team with the purpose of providing technical expertise and training to the other court administration teams. Their former work was built around the control and coordination tasks that the teams would now be doing for themselves. As the former supervisors were determining how they should be organised to get their work done, one of them realised, out loud, that once everyone on the other teams had developed their skills to the expert level, this team could be out of work and out of jobs.

At first, there was a bit of 'Poor us, this redesign stuff is a way to get rid of supervisors. How can *they* do this to us?' Then people got to work, brainstorming ways that they could add value to the court by providing the needed technical expertise and training. They began to call themselves the Resources Team and visited each of the court administration teams to find out what other services, besides training, they might like to have. The new Resources Team asked the chief deputy to consult with them during the workshop. They interviewed her in depth about special projects and research opportunities in their court.

This entrepreneurial spirit caught on and they began to develop a marketing plan for the services they were going to offer the court. As a result, the case backlog was dealt with in two months. The court administration teams were able to get the support they needed to get all team members cross trained in less than a year. Many special projects, that had been put on hold, were either completed or scheduled into the work of the Resources Team.

'Really, Mary, we WANT you to resign – we don't need a supervisor anymore!'

One of the teams going through redesign in a U.S. district court office had a supervisor who had just returned from maternity leave. As this group of women was going through the different parts of the redesign workshop, they found that their supervisor seemed to be struggling with what her role would be in the new design. Mary was well liked by all the members and they wanted to make sure that she had work that was meaningful to her in the new design, even though they would be sharing many of the supervisory tasks that she was used to doing. Mary also appeared to be very emotional on several occasions, which many of the other team members, having had babies themselves, understood to be post-partum depression.

Finally, one of the team members turned to her and said, 'Would you like to stay home with your baby for a while? I know this means resigning, but it seems like you start crying every time we talk about your work.'

The team spent quite a bit of time helping Mary sort out her feelings about working and not working. At the end of the day, she said that she would talk this over with her husband that night and thanked the team for their understanding and their help with this issue.

The next morning, the team jumped right back into the discussion of what was right for Mary to do. She said that she and her husband had agreed that it would be good for her to leave the court and be at work home with the new baby and their toddler. She was reluctant to commit to this. Then, an intuitive team member said, 'Really, Mary, we want you to resign – we don't need a supervisor anymore. You have taken really good care of us. Now it is time for us to take care of ourselves. We really appreciate all you have done for us, now do something for yourself.' Mary realised that she had been taking care of the team and a wonderful discussion of how they were now ready to take care of themselves took place. What they all realised was that in this new self managing workplace they were all designing; there would be resources and supports in place to help them if things got a bit bumpy. And Mary realised that the team members were ready to take care of each other.

'Just lock us in a room and we will come out two teams!'

A large U.S. district court decided to implement the Team Based Management program. The largest branch, including the central administrative offices, redesigned first. Then redesign came to one of the smaller branches.

During the design phase of a workshop, 26 people decided that the best way to organise their work was to be in two cross functional teams. After listing the work each team would do, the skills and knowledge that would be needed by each team, and how many people needed on a team, the group ran into quite a controversy over how to determine who would be on each team. They knew who had what skill and knowledge, but that did not seem to be the way to divide up. There was a mysterious undercurrent to the discussion.

After going around and around a few times, one brave soul said, 'Here is our problem: There are two slackers in this group and no one wants them to be on their team. We all know who they are and we know how they have been able to hide their slacking off from management.' (Two people were red faced.)

Another group member suggested that if they did not divide themselves up, management would probably do it for them. The group decided that it would be better if they took care of this themselves. 'After all, this is what self management is about. If we can't do this, how can we possibly handle the hard stuff?' So, the group asked to be sequestered in the jury room (how appropriate) and to be left alone until they were finished with the team assignments.

Time passed. Occasional loud voices could be heard. Someone came out, walked swiftly to their desk, and returned to the jury room with a box of tissues. More loud voices. The court manager paced in the hallway. Two hours, word came from the jury room – 'We are almost there.' Another half hour, and, voilà, two teams emerged from the room. People were obviously worn out. However, the teams were very satisfied with their ability to deal with a difficult problem, work out conflicts amongst themselves, and stick with a problem until it was solved. They also felt that the team assignments would be successful because they had worked so hard to get them right in the beginning.

Headline: 'Probation Officers to Share Cases'

Federal probation officers are responsible for supervising people who are sentenced to probation by federal judges. They monitor their clients' adherence to conditions set by the court, such as employment, travel restrictions, payment of restitution, counseling and treatment. The probation officers make periodic reports to the court on their clients' compliance with their terms of probation.

For people outside of probation work, the above headline may not appear too startling. However, for those who are familiar with the world of probation, this is a major shift in thinking. It did happen, in a redesign workshop with a group of federal probation officers.

Traditionally, probation officers are fairly possessive about the cases that they are assigned to manage. There may be discussion between officers on ways to handle certain situations, resources available for various clients, and the like. But, each officer takes responsibility, solely, for the clients on her / his caseload. During a conversation on how to re-organise themselves around their work, a group of federal probation officers began to talk about the possibility of sharing cases.

In the new design, the officers decided that each team should take collective responsibility for all of the cases that had been assigned to its members. New case assignments would go to the team, rather than a specific officer. The team provides total services for its assigned clients and to the court, from beginning to end of the probation sentence.

As these probation officers work in a region that is sparsely populated with large distances between towns, sharing cases provides an important benefit to their clients and the court. If one officer were to go out on site visits (home or work), they could visit all the clients in a particular area, rather than just the ones on her or his caseload. While one officer is out of the office, any issues that arise with their clients could be handled by the officers in the office. In this way the number of site visits per client increases, travel becomes more efficient and effective, and there is always someone available in the office that is familiar with the clients and the caseloads.

And in another Federal Probation Office . . . 'Who needs a middle manager?'

At the time of the redesign workshop in this federal probation office, the deputy chief probation officer position was vacant. In the course of the workshop, the participants decided to tackle the topic of what to do with this open position. The chief deputy job had been used in the past as a promotional opportunity for probation officers with lots of seniority, as well as managing the daily operations of the office.

The probation officers and the chief probation officer began to examine the work that had been done by the former chief deputy. They discovered that a lot of the work was now going to be done by the new self managing teams. After taking this work into consideration, there was not much left over. Most of this was in the area of coordination between various field offices. It did not appear to be enough to warrant a full time person. The chief probation officer said that if they could figure out a way to handle the coordination issues, he would consider hiring another field officer rather than a manager.

As a result of this discussion, a coordination council was created. Each team would send one member to a meeting, once a month, with the chief probation officer. The purpose of the monthly meeting was to: share information across field office and central office boundaries; monitor the strategic plan and budget for the region; review progress on goals; and make decisions that affected the office as a whole. Membership on the council would rotate, every few months, with the terms staggered so that there would be some continuity from one meeting to the next. Processes were developed for information

251

Chapter 16
Stories from
Workplace
Redesign
Experiences

sharing, conflict management, and decision making between the regular meetings. Emergency meetings could be called when necessary. They decided to use telecommunications technology during winter and other times when travel was too hazardous for people to get to the meeting site.

'Now I see where my work fits into the big picture'

A middle aged man decided to go to work for the federal government. He was tired of working really hard and had heard the rumour that federal employees did not have to work very hard. He found what he thought was an easy, no sweat job in a federal court office, in the filing room. He felt he had no accountability or responsibility. 'Who cares about filing? It is not that important' and 'the supervisor takes the flack'.

Shortly after he was hired, the court office decided to become a self managing workplace. Time was spent educating all staff, managers and workers, on what this might mean for them and getting them ready for the actual redesign of their workplace. This man thought he could coast through this and keep his low stress job just the way it was.

During the redesign workshop, this man decided to be quiet and go along with whatever the majority of his co-workers wanted to do. After the redesign of the office, rather than being in the filing room, this man found himself on a case administration team. His duties were going to expand from simply filing papers, to all of the work involved in the life cycle of federal court cases. He was not very pleased with this development, but wanted to stay with the court office, so went along with it.

As the team began to implement their new design, they discovered that they had a team member who did not want to do anything but file. A critical part of their design was that all team members would be cross trained so they could do all of the work of the team. The team began to work with this man, so that he too would be able to do all of the tasks required by their work. The team wisely decided to start by educating him on where their work fitted into the 'big picture' of the court system.

One of his first learning opportunities was to follow some cases from beginning to end. He worked at the front window and learned all of the intricacies of intake when people file cases for the court to hear. He chose several cases to follow. He then began learning all of the rest that was involved in moving a case through the court system.

One day he found himself working in the courtroom during a hearing. He noticed that the judge was shuffling through papers on the bench and getting red in the face. After several minutes of this, the judge bellowed, 'I AM SO TIRED OF FILES THAT HAVE DOCUMENTS OUT OF ORDER AND MISSING. How can I run a court and handle cases well if I don't have the information I need in the file?' He then called a recess and called the clerk of the court (top manager) into his chambers. The clerk wisely called this man and his team into chambers with him.

This man learned that because a critical document was missing – had possibly been misfiled by him – the case could be postponed. The next available hearing date on the judge's calendar was over two months away. With his newly acquired learning, this man thought about the defendant in the case having to sit two more months without resolution, the increased attorney's fees, and the additional burden on an already overloaded court calendar. He also remembered that part of the agreement that he and the others in the office had been to take responsibility for their work being completed in a timely and correct manner. He asked the judge to continue the recess for an hour to give the team a chance to go find the missing document. The judge agreed. Fortunately, a team member found the misfiled document within the hour and the hearing went on as planned.

This man said he learned an important lesson that day. 'Now I see where my work fits into the big picture. I am glad that the team 'forced' me to learn about the rest of the work. And my work is much more meaningful and satisfying now than it was before.'

Workshop managers transform, too

People who manage redesign workshops find that they transform, too, just being part of the process. As one man said so well: 'This way of treating people, as if they are intelligent and thoughtful, has changed my life. I find myself treating my family differently, even my children. I used to always assume that I have to tell them what to do, to give them answers to their questions, that Dad always knows best. Now I see them as thinking, creative, talented people who can often figure out their own best answer. I can engage them in conversations about what is right and what is wrong. I find that I am learning from them. We have such a different relationship now, much more open and close. They have told me that they appreciate how they can now talk with me on topics that they used to avoid bringing up. This has been so good for me, at home and at work.'

I did not work alone in these various workshops and would like to mention people who were also involved in this challenging and satisfying work:

> Kathleen Alston, Joe Barclay, Janet Bubnis,
> Ken Delaporte, Salome de Beers, Don Dodds,
> Helena Dolny, Jennifer du Preez, Clifford Fewel,
> Richard Heltzel, David Hendrickson, Nancy Intermill,
> Fredericka Joyner, Beth Macy, Bankies Malan,
> Douglas Meyer, Bette Niedbalski, Shannon O'Brien,
> Bob Rehm, Pat Sandlin, Norm Sherman,
> and Mary Fewel Tulin.

Nancy Cebula is an independent consultant who works with organisations and communities in the public and private sectors, helping them discover ways to become successful in our turbulent environment through participative planning, design, and learning.

E-mail: participate@earthlink.net

Chapter Notes

Chapter 1

1 The two design principles were first developed by Fred Emery as a result of his action research in the British coal mines and the Norwegian Workplace Democracy Projects. This description of the design principles and the characteristics of self managing workplaces is adapted from the book, *Participative Design for Participative Democracy,* edited by M. Emery, Centre for Continuing Education, The Australian National University, 1993.

2 Model adapted from Fred Emery, 'Light on the Hill,' in *Participative Design for Participative Democracy.*

3 For more on Barry Oshry see his book, *Seeing Systems: Unlocking the Mysteries of Organizational Life,* Berrett-Koehler Publishers, 1995.

Chapter 2

1 Quote from *The Fragile Species,* by Lewis Thomas.

2 This story comes from my experience doing workplace redesign at StorageTek with my partner Gary Frank. StorageTek is a corporation that makes information storage systems. This story is documented by Blue Sky Productions in its workplace video, 'Cutting Edge Teamwork.'

Chapter 3

1 Adapted from Kurt Lewin's report that he co-authored with Ron Lippitt and Ralph White, *Patterns of Aggressive Behaviour in Experimentally Created Social Climates*, Journal of Social Psychology, 1939.

2 For more on Kurt Lewin's contributions to workplace democracy see Alfred Marrow's biography, *The Practical Theorist*, Basic Books, 1969.

3 Adapted from Kurt Lewin's chapter, 'The Practicality of Democracy,' in G. Murphy (ed.), *Human Nature and Enduring Peace*, Houghton-Miflin, 1945.

4 I combined two stories here. One is the pub story Fred Emery told me. The other is based on the research paper, 'Alternative Work Organizations,' by Eric Trist and others in the book, *The Social Engagement of Social Science: A Tavistock Anthology; The Socio-technical Perspective*, University of Pennsylvania Press, 1993.

5 The best source of information on the history of workplace design is Marvin Weisbord's classic book, *Productive Workplaces*, Jossey-Bass Publishers, 1988.

Chapter 5

1 Adapted from the writings of Fred and Merrelyn Emery. See the book, *Participative Design for Participative Democracy*, edited by Merrelyn Emery, for more detail about concepts and theory. The participative design workshop was developed in Australia in the early 1970s by Fred Emery, Merrelyn Emery, and Alan Davies.

Chapter 7

1 For information about search conferences see 'Search Conferences for Participative Planning' by Robert Rehm and Nancy Cebula, available through Hawthorn Press.

2 Quote from *The New Russians* by Hedrick Smith, Random House, N.Y., 1990.

3 Quote from Howard Zinn, *You Can't Be Neutral on a Moving Train.*

4 For more on Christopher Alexander's architectural principles see his book, *A Timeless Way of Building,* Oxford University Press, 1979.

Chapter 8

1 I wrote this guide for the Land Bank of South Africa and REA Consulting to support the new self managing teams in the branch banks. Portions of the guide were adapted from *Participative Design for Participative Democracy.* And some parts are from the Fast Cycle Full Participation Work Systems Design method that I created with Gary Frank and Bill Pasmore.

Chapter 11

1 The quotes are from the videotape 'Team Based Management' done for the FJC by Allan Kobernick of Blue Sky Productions.

2 The Team Based Management project was started by Barbara Anderson, Chief of In Court Programs for the Federal Judicial Center. Here are the names of the facilitators we have worked with: Kathleen Alston, Janet Bubnis, Mike Dobbins, Richard Heltzel, Julie Morse, Ted McGregor, Shannon O'Brien, Bruce Rifkin, Pat Sandlin, Norm Sherman,

and Michael Thompson. All the facilitators are managers from various federal court organisations around the USA.

Chapter 13

1 Fred Emery originated a theory on what staff want. His work is cited by Frank Heckman, 'Designing Organizations for Flow Experiences'. *Journal of Quality and Participation,* 20 (March 1997): 31.

2 Charles Handy describes the sigmoidal curve theory of organizational ups and downs, that after 20 or so years every organization must 'reinvent' itself or begin skidding down the downward slope. See his *Age of Paradox,* (Boston: Harvard Business School Press, 1995), pp.49-67.

Chapter 14

1 Nic Turner joined DIA in 1992 as Organisation Development Manager, and in 1993 persuaded the directors that coaching, upward appraisal and feedback would help bring about the desired change in culture. He became a mentor to Mal Tanner and his colleagues, developing a process consultancy capability within Personnel and Training. Shortly before moving to Boots, Nic introduced Mal to self management.

Beesley, Jacqueline, (1998) *The Way Forward – the Impact of Management as Team Leaders in a Participative Workplace Democracy,* Dissertation for MA in HRM, Oxford Brookes University.

Do It All opts for DIY management, feature article in IRS Employment Trends 664 September 1998.

Resources and Contacts for Participative Design and Open Systems Work

Participative Planning, Design and Learning

The world is turbulent and unpredictable. Successful organisations, therefore, need to understand this changing world so that they can plan effectively and re-design themselves. This creates the capacity for adaptive strategic planning and adaptive organisational structures so as to take advantage of change, and deliver high performance.

We offer consultancy and training services to organisations and communities, so that people have the tools and processes to plan what they want, and how to redesign thair ways of working to achieve their objectives.

The following introductory workshop is offered, and can be re-designed depending on the question and the needs.

Using the Search Conference and Participative Design
for co-creating outstanding, results, learning and performance

Why Participative Planning and Design?

People want to learn, contribute and work together for a successful future. Engaging them in planning what they want and how to achieve it, results in improved solutions, performance, results and learning. Approaches such as the Search Conference and Participative Design offer proven ways for people to get energetic, excited and effective at planning together for their future. This workshop offers the chance to consider these two simple (yet not easy) processes for your tool kit.

Building the capacity to adapt

The underlying principle that informs these two approaches is Open Systems Theory. This states that for an organisation (group, department, community, team, etc) to thrive in turbulent times, it needs to have a direct and open relationship with its environment. This enables it to:

   i)   get feedback about what is going on;
   ii) use this feedback to proactively plan and adapt to new and future requirements.

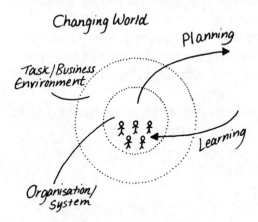

The Search Conference, which is a simple yet profound low tech-planning tool, enables people to make a plan for their most desirable future. Typical applications include strategic, unit, project, merger and partnership planning. It can be applied to any group, in private, public, not-for-profit or community setting. It was invented by Eric Trist, Fred and Merrelyn Emery.

Participative Design is a tool for re-designing organisations to be self managing, so that control and co-ordination are carried out by the people doing the work. As with Search this can be applied to any setting where people need to get organised to do the work.

These approaches build in the adaptive and proactive planning mechanisms that organisations need to continually re-invent themselves in the face of increasingly turbulent times.

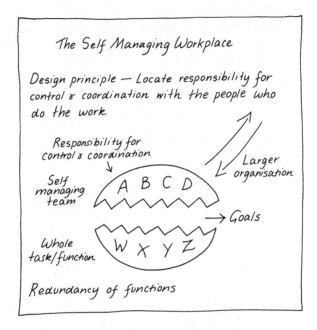

Workshop objectives

The workshop will be a mixture of practise, theory and applications. Participants will experience each method step by step, debriefing as we go. This will enable you to:

1 Learn the principles for designing and leading Search Conferences and Participative Design

2. Experience some of the methods such as 'Keep, drop and create' and 'The six criteria for productive work'

3. Apply the methods to real cases

```
Six Criteria for
Productive Work

(1) Elbow room for
        decision making
(2) Ongoing learning
(3) Variety
(4) Mutual support & respect
(5) Meaningfulness
(6) Desirable future
```

The audience

The workshop is for facilitators, managers, change agents, administrators, community leaders – for anyone in the private, voluntary or statutory sectors concerned with change, strategic planning, organisation development and learning.

Workshop leaders

Martin Large facilitates search conferences and participative design workshops in the private, public and community sectors. He has consulted in organisation development for over 20 years and works for the Gloucestershire Vision-21 Facilitators Learning Network.

E-mail: Mhclarge@aol.com
Tel: 01453 757040

Outline:

The Search Conference
- Expectations, Purpose and Agenda
- Overview of SC and PD
- SCI – Scanning and Analysing the Environment
  - Desirable and probable futures of the world
  - Events and trends affecting our system
- SCII – Systems Analysis
  - What is our story? Our common history?
  - What should we keep, drop and create?
  - Our most desirable future
- SCIII – Adaptive Planning and Dissemination
  - Dealing with constraints
  - Action planning
  - Dissemination
- Preparing for and Conducting a Search Conference

Participative Design
- Overview and Principles – Assessment of Current Structure
- Six Criteria for Effective Work
- Democratic and Bureaucratic Design Principles
- Assessing Current Structure and Work Flow
- Redesign
- Preparing for PD
- Evaluation and Follow Up

Participative Planning, Design and Learning
Hawthorn House, 1 Lansdown Lane, Stroud
Gloucestershire, GL5 1BJ, Britain.

Tel: (01453) 757040
Fax: (01453) 751138
E-mail: Mhclarge@aol.com
www.hawthornpress.com

Resources
and
Contacts

Nancy Cebula and Bob Rehm
1460 Judson Drive
Boulder, Colorado 80303

People
In
Charge

Tel: 303 499 1607
Fax: 303 494 2337
E-mail: participate@earthlink.net

Fran Ryan
Fran Ryan is an Organisation Psychologist working in organisation development at The Prudential, and is currently engaged in introducing self-managing teams using Participative Design in a customer servicing business.

Tel: 44 (0) 589 209448 (M)
Tel: 44 (0) 1865 395636 (H)
E-mail: fran.ryan@prudential.co.uk
        fran@ryanmcphail.demon.co.uk

RGA Consulting
P O Box 12808, Clubview 0014
Republic of South Africa

Tel: (012) 654-1236/0110
Fax: (012) 654 1236
E-mail: bttcon@icon.co.za

Ecology of Work Conferences

Ecology of Work Conferences feature innovations in union-management cooperation, work redesign, and employee involvement to create high performing organizations.

Eberhard Köhler & Kevin P. O'Kelly
Research Managers and Conference Coordinators – Europe
The European Foundation
Wyattville Road
Loughlinstown
Co. Dublin, Ireland

Tel: +353 1 204 3100
Fax: +353 1 282 6456
E-mail: eberhard.kohler@eurofound.ie
        Kevin.Okelly@eurofound.ie

Tom Chase
Executive Director and Conference Coordinator – USA
The Ecology of Work
306 Catamount Road
Northwood,
NH, USA 03261

Tel: +1 603 942 8189
Fax: +1 603 942 8190
E-mail: ecowork@cssunltd.com

Amerin Consulting Group Pty Ltd

Peter Aughton and Sam Joukadjian
We are a team of management and organisational consultants who apply the Open Systems Theory approach to help organisations become responsive and adaptive and achieve high levels of performance.

People
In
Charge

Suite 5, Level 7
14 Queen's Road,
Melbourne
Victoria, Australia 3004

Tel: 61 3 9820 9122
Fax: 61 3 9820 1553
E-mail: melboffice@amerin.com.au
www.amerin.com.au

Fred Emery Institute Ltd

Mission: To bring into being participative democratic structures – developing people, communities, organisations and societies.

The Fred Emery Institute was formed to translate open systems theory into practise, educate people in OST, to conduct research and to undertake special projects. Merrelyn Emery, who has researched and developed OST over many years, can be reached via the Institute.

Contact: via Amerin address above.

E-mail: admin@fredemery.com.au
www.fredemery.com.au

Other Books from Hawthorn Press

Confronting Conflict
A first-aid kit for handling conflict
Friedrich Glasl

Conflict costs! When tensions and differences are ignored they grow into conflicts, injuring relationships, groups and organisations. So, how can we tackle conflict successfully?

Dr Friedrich Glasl has worked with conflict resolution in companies, schools and communities for over 30 years, earning him and his techniques enormous respect.

Confronting Conflict is authoritative and up to date, containing new examples, exercises theory and techniques. You can start by assessing the symptoms and causes of conflict, and ask, 'Am I fanning the flames?' And then consider, 'How can I behave constructively rather than attack or avoid others?'

Here are tools to; Analyse symptoms, types, causes of conflict, hot or cold, personal chemistry, structures or environment; understand how temperaments affect conflicts; acknowledge when you have a conflict, understand conflict escalation, how to lessen conflict through changing behaviour, attitudes and perceptions; practise developing considerate confrontation, seizing golden moments, and strengthening empathy.

Confronting Conflict will be useful for managers, facilitators, management lecturers and professionals such as teachers and community workers, mediators and workers in dispute resolution.

Dr Friedrich Glasl is a recognised authority on conflict. His PhD was on conflict prevention and peace building. He worked for the Dutch NPI for Organisational Development from 1967, and has lectured in conflict at Salzburg University since 1985. He has written many books, including *Enterprise of the Future*.

192pp; 216 x 138mm; paperback; 1 869 890 71 X

Navigator
Men's Development Workbook
James Traeger, Jenny Daisley and Liz Willis

Navigator is one of the very first personal and professional development workbooks in the UK specifically developed for all men at work, on their own or in relationships and as fathers and sons. Life for men is changing, and changing fast. Many men are asking who they are and where they, and their expectations of life, fit in with these rapid changes. *Navigator* provides individual men with a down-to-earth way of tackling many of these issues.

Navigator forms the basis of a 3 month Men's Development Programme recently researched and piloted inside a wide range of UK organisations, including BT Mobile, Braintree District Council, Midland Bank, NatWest UK, Wolverhampton MBC, The University of Cambridge and The University of London.

Navigator is full of positive thinking and good humour and is packed with ideas, examples and practical exercises with the points illustrated with cartoons and real case studies. Contents include; realistic self-assessment; challenging expectations; a man's world, clarifying values; taking risks and making changes; physical and feelings fitness; setting a goal strategy that works; assertiveness for men; putting yourself across.

288pp; 297 x 210mm; paperback; 1 869 890 80 9

Workways: Seven Stars to Steer By
Biography Workbook for Building a More Enterprising Life
Kees Locher and Jos van der Brug

This biography workbook helps you consider your working life, and make more conscious choices, at a time of great change in our 'workways'. Background readings, thirty seven exercises and creative activities are carefully structured for individuals or self-help groups.

352pp; 297 x 210mm; paperback; 1 869 890 89 2

Springboard
Women's Development
Workbook
Liz Willis and Jenny Daisley

Winner for the BBC of the 1989 Lady Platt Award for Innovative Equal Opportunities Training and the 1993 National Training Award.

A practical self-development workbook, designed for women to work through themselves or in a training group, *Springboard's* reputation continues to grow.

Packed with exercises and real-life examples, it is down-to-earth, positive and practical. The workbook is used by many large companies in their training schemes for women, and has sold over 100,000 copies to date.

4th Edition; 288pp; 297 x 210mm; illustrations, cartoons; paperback;
1 869 890 69 8

Soul Weaving
How to shape your destiny and inspire your dreams
Betty Staley

Soul Weaving is an invitation to weave a design for the Soul's journey bringing together the colours and textures of our personality to reveal pattern and meaning. *Soul Weaving* is the most comprehensive introduction to the temperaments, archetypes and soul qualities, as defined by Rudolf Steiner, which enable us to better understand ourselves and our relationship to the world.

This book shows us how to; transform our temperament; realise and integrate our soul type; understand the influences of the archetypal points of view; make life changes such as choosing a spiritual path, living in balance, cultivating the power of love, and much more.

Betty Staley's interest in psychology started at graduate school in the 1950's and has never left her. She has taught for over 30 years in

Steiner Waldorf schools and lectures at Rudolf Steiner College, Sacramento. A companion to *Tapestries, Soul Weaving* is a lively and authoritative introduction to spiritual psychology. Betty is also the author of the best seller *Between Form and Freedom – a practical guide to the teenage years,* which has been translated into Dutch, German and Japanese.

Whilst an accessible Mind/Body/Spirit or Psychology and Self-Help book, *Soul Weaving* will interest counsellors, teachers, educators, doctors, humanistic and transpersonal students and facilitators.

240pp; 216 x 138mm; paperback; 1 869 890 05 1

Tapestries
Weaving Life's Journey
Betty Staley

Tapestries gives a moving and wise guide to women's life phases. Drawing on original biographies of a wide variety of women, informed by personal experience and by her understanding of anthroposophy, Betty Staley offers a vivid account of life journeys. This book helps readers reflect on their own lives and prepare for the next step in weaving their own biographical tapestry.

336pp; 216 x 138mm; paperback; 1 869 890 15 9

Manhood
An action plan for changing men's lives
Steve Biddulph

Most men don't have a life. So begins the most powerful, practical and honest book ever to be written about men and boys. Not about our problems – but about how we can find the joy and energy of being in a male body with a man's mind and spirit – about men's liberation.

Steve Biddulph, author of *Raising Boys* and the million-seller *The Secret of Happy Children,* writes about the turning point that men have reached – as reflected in films like *The Full Monty.* He gives practical personal answers to how things can be different from the bedroom to the workplace. He tells powerful stories about healing the rift between fathers and sons. About friendship. How women and men can get along in dynamic harmonious ways. How boys can be raised to be healthy men.

Manhood has had a profound emotional impact on tens of thousands of readers worldwide, and has been passed from son to father, friend to friend, husband to wife, with the simple message 'you must read this!'

*'Steve Biddulph should be in the UK what he is in Australia, **the** household name in the business of raising boys and being a man.'*
Dorothy Rowe, psychologist and writer

272pp; 216 x 138mm; 12 black and white photographs; paperback; 1 869 890 99 X

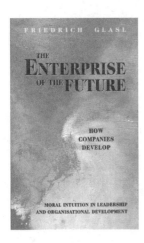

The Enterprise of the Future
Moral Intuition in Leadership and Organisational Development
Friedrich Glasl

Friedrich Glasl looks at the future role of the organisation in the community, and the opportunity it offers for personal development. He addresses the need to expand consciousness beyond the organisation to the 'shared destiny' it holds with the community and with whom it shares a common enterprise.

160pp; 216 x 138mm; paperback; 1 869 890 79 5

Money for a Better World
Rudolf Mees

This slim volume re-works our attitudes towards handling money and presents finance on a human scale. It discusses alternative ways of looking at money in our modern world and realistic methods of approaching borrowing, saving and lending.

64pp; 216 x 138mm; paperback; 1 869 890 26 4

Vision in Action
Working with Soul and Spirit in Small Organisations
Christopher Schaefer, Tÿno Voors

This second edition has been thoroughly revised and updated for the 1990's. *Vision in Action* is a workbook for those involved in social creation – in collaborative deeds that can influence the social environment in which we live and where our ideas and actions can matter. This is a user-friendly, hands-on guide for developing healthy small organisations – organisations with soul and spirit.

256pp; 235 x 152mm; paperback; 1 869 890 88 4

Ordering books

If you have difficulty ordering Hawthorn Press books from a bookshop, you can order direct from:
Scottish Book Source, 137 Dundee Street,
Edinburgh, EH11 1BG
Tel: (0131) 229 6800   Fax: (0131) 229 9070
E-mail: scotbook@globalnet.co.uk

(Payment with order please, by credit card or sterling cheque.)

All Hawthorn Press titles are available from:

Anthroposophic Press, 3390 Route 9, Hudson, NY 12534
Tel: (518) 851 2054   Fax: (518) 851 2047
E-mail: anthropres@aol.com
www.anthropress.org

Astam Books Pty Ltd, 57-61 John Street, Leichhardt,
NSW 204
Tel: (02) 9566 4400   Fax: (02) 9566 4411
E-mail: sales@astambooks.com.au

Peter Hyde Assoc. (Pty) Ltd. PO Box 2856,
Capetown 8000, South Africa
Tel: (21) 422 6692   Fax: (21) 422 0375
E-mail: peter.hyde@icelogic.co.za

Ordering *People In Charge* in bulk orders for organisations:

BRITAIN

Hawthorn Press, 1 Lansdown Lane, Stroud,
Gloucestershire, GL5 1BJ, United Kingdom
Tel: (01453) 757040   Fax: (01453) 751138
E-mail: hawthornpress@hawthornpress.com
www.hawthornpress.com

USA / NORTH AMERICA
Nancy Cebula and Bob Rehm
E-mail: participate@earthlink.net